Houston Astros 2019

A Baseball Companion

Edited by Patrick Dubuque, Aaron Gleeman and Bret Sayre

Baseball Prospectus

Craig Brown and Dave Pease, Consultant Editors
Rob McQuown and Harry Pavlidis, Statistics Editors

Copyright © 2019 by DIY Baseball, LLC.
All rights reserved

This book or any part thereof may not be reproduced or transmitted in any form or by any means, electronic or mechanical, including photocopying, recording, or by any information storage and retrieval system, without permission in writing from the publisher.

Limit of Liability/Disclaimer of Warranty: While the publisher and the author have used their best efforts in preparing this book, they make no representations or warranties with respect to the accuracy or completeness of the contents of this book and specifically disclaim any implied warranties of merchantability or fitness for a particular purpose. No warranty may be created or extended by sales representatives or written sales materials. The advice and strategies contained herein may not be suitable for your situation. You should consult with a professional where appropriate. Neither the publisher nor the author shall be liable for any loss of profit or any other commercial damages, including but not limited to special, incidental, consequential, or other damages.

Library of Congress Cataloging-in-Publication Data:
paperback
ISBN-13: 978-1-949332-10-0

Project Credits
Cover Design: Kathleen Dyson
Interior Design and Production: Jeff Pease, Dave Pease
Layout: Jeff Pease, Dave Pease

Baseball icon courtesy of Uberux, from https://www.shareicon.net/author/uberux

Ballpark diagram courtesy of Lou Spirito/THIRTY81 Project, https://thirty81project.com/

Manufactured in the United States of America
10 9 8 7 6 5 4 3 2 1

Table of Contents

Foreword v
    Rob Mains

Statistical Introduction vii

Part 1: Team Analysis

Table for Two: Previewing the 2019 Houston Astros 3
    Wilson Karaman and Rob Mains

Performance Graphs 7

2018 Team Performance 8

2019 Team Projections 9

Team Personnel 10

Minute Maid Park Stats 11

Astros Team Analysis 13

Part 2: Player Analysis

Astros Player Analysis 18

Astros Prospects 93

Part 3: Featured Articles

The Hole in The Shift is Fixing Itself 107
    Russell Carleton

The State of the Quality Start 111
    Rob Mains

Heads-Up Hacking—The First Pitch 117
    Matthew Trueblood

A Hymn for the Index Stat 123
    Patrick Dubuque

Index of Names 127

Foreword

Rob Mains

Welcome to this companion of the 2019 Houston Astros. We at Baseball Prospectus are excited to provide this analysis of the Astros.

Our website, Baseball Prospectus, is a leader in delivering high-quality commentary and data to baseball fans everywhere. To some, those words—commentary and data—appear mutually exclusive. There are people out there who believe that traditional analysis and advanced analytics must run on different paths. But the simplistic narrative of stats vs. traditionalists just isn't true. Every team's analytics department interacts with scouting, development, and major league operations with a common goal: Delivering a championship. New technologies, like radar tracking of pitch speeds and movement, enable talent evaluators to focus on qualitative aspects of pitching like mechanics and pitch sequencing. In-game strategies like infield shifts, based on batters' hit tendencies, help turn balls in play into outs. Hitters use information to adjust their swings to maximize run production.

All these numbers can seem, at best, intimidating, and at worst, counterproductive to the casual fan. Even as technology and analysis have embedded themselves deeply into the way teams run, it can often feel like statistics create a displacement between the viewer and the sport, breaking them out of the action. And yet every fan incorporates the numbers to some degree; stats like batting average and earned run average, so fundamental to how we talk about performance, are actually complicated formulas. They don't bother people because those formulas have become second nature, as easy to translate as the action on the field.

Along the way, new statistics have entered baseball's lexicon. You'll see some of them, like on-base percentage (which measures a batter's ability to get on base via walk, hit batter, or hit), OPS (on-base plus slugging), and average exit velocity (the speed of balls off a hitter's bat) on broadcasts. Others, like DRC+, might well be new to you. Some of them have been well-defined to the public, others haven't. That lack of context has created ambiguity. Fans know that a ball hit 100 mph is scorched, but does that mean extra bases? (Not if it's hit on the ground or high in the air it doesn't.)

For those who are amenable to them, the new statistics can increase the enjoyment and understanding of the game. They can help fans identify when a pitcher is tiring, when a stolen base or a bunt attempt makes sense (and, more often, when it doesn't), or how a team's lineup might be constructed. Websites like Baseball Prospectus add to that understanding by weaving metrics into the narrative of the game. That's the goal of this publication: to take some of the newer, more complicated statistics and make them as intuitive as the ones on the back of old baseball cards.

But you don't need to love analytics to love baseball. The fans at BP who worked together to write this guide are captivated first and foremost by the game itself. We're drawn to Aaron Judge's power, Francisco Lindor's glove, Billy Hamilton's speed and Patrick Corbin's slider and don't need numbers to tell us why they're so mesmerizing. The underlying statistics provide depth to the game that we all love.

We hope you'll find that this guide helps you better understand the Astros. Our analysts have studied the team's major league personnel and its minor league affiliates to identify their strengths and weaknesses, both the obvious ones and those that only a careful dissection of players' performances—yes, including the data—can reveal. You don't need us to tell you who was good and who wasn't in 2018, but our models and writers can help you project how each player is going to perform this year and beyond, and appreciate the greatness of each new game as it unfolds. As in the sport itself, the human and analytic components combine to generate a deeper overall understanding.

Think back to the first time you saw a baseball game on a high-definition TV. You'd grown familiar with how the game looked and felt on a picture tube. But new TV allowed you to see details that you'd never seen before. That's how advanced statistics work. The game itself is why you're here and why you're buying this. (And, for that matter, why we wrote it.) The statistical measures provide the sharper focus, the detail, the depth of knowledge that you didn't have before, generating an overall superior picture. Enjoy the view.

—*Rob Mains is an author of Baseball Prospectus.*

Statistical Introduction

Sports are, fundamentally, a blend of athletic endeavor and storytelling. Baseball, like any other sport, tells its stories in so many ways: in the arc of a game from the stands or a season from the box scores, in photos, or even in numbers. At Baseball Prospectus, we understand that statistics don't replace observation or any of baseball's stories, but complement everything else that makes the game so much fun.

What stats help us with is with patterns and precision, variance and value. This book can help you learn things you may not see from watching a game or hundred, whether it's the path of a career over time or the breadth of the entire MLB. We'd also never ask you to choose between our numbers and the experience of viewing a game from the cheap seats or the comfort of your home; our publication combines running the numbers with observations and wisdom from some of the brightest minds we can find. But if you *do* want to learn more about the numbers beyond what's on the backs of player jerseys, let us help explain.

Offense

At the end of this past year, we've revised our methodology for determining batting value. Long-time readers of Baseball Prospectus will notice that we've retired True Average in favor of a new metric: Deserved Runs Created Plus (DRC+). Developed by Jonathan Judge and our stats team, this statistic measures everything a player does at the plate–reaching base, hitting for power, making outs, and moving runners over–and puts it on a scale where 100 equals league-average performance. A DRC+ of 150 is terrific, a DRC+ of 100 is average, and a DRC+ of 75 means you better be an excellent defender.

DRC+ also does a better job than any of our previous metrics in taking contextual factors into account. The model adjusts for how the park affects performance, but also for things like the talent of the opposing pitcher, value of different types of batted-ball events, league, temperature, and other factors. It's able to describe a player's expected offensive contribution than any other statistic we've found over the years, and also does a better job of predicting future performance as well.

The other aspect of run-scoring is baserunning, which we quantify using Baserunning Runs. BRR not only records the value of stolen bases (or getting caught in the act), but also accounts for a runner's ability to go first to third on a single or advance on a fly ball.

Defense

Where offensive value is *relatively* easy to identify and understand, defensive value is ... not. Over the past dozen years, the sabermetric community has focused mostly on stats based on zone data: a real-live human person records the type of batted ball and estimated landing location, and models are created that give expected outs. From there, you can compare fielders' actual outs to those expected ones. Simple, right?

Unfortunately, zone data has two major issues. First, zone data is recorded by commercial data providers who keep the raw data private unless you pay for it. (All the statistics we build in this book and on our website use public data as inputs.) That hurts our ability to test assumptions or duplicate results. Second, over the years it has become apparent that there's quite a bit of "noise" in zone-based fielding analysis. Sometimes the conclusions drawn from zone data don't hold up to scrutiny, and sometimes the different data provided by different providers don't look anything alike, giving wildly different results. Sometimes the hard-working professional stringers or scorers might unknowingly inflict unconscious bias into the mix: for example good fielders will often be credited with more expected outs despite the data, and ballparks with high press boxes tend to score more line drives than ones with a lower press box.

Enter our Fielding Runs Above Average (FRAA). For most positions, FRAA is built from play-by-play data, which allows us to avoid the subjectivity found in many other fielding metrics. The idea is this: count how many fielding plays are made by a given player and compare that to expected plays for an average fielder at their position (based on pitcher ground-ball tendencies and batter handedness). Then we adjust for park and base-out situations.

When it comes to catchers, our methodology is a little different thanks to the laundry list of responsibilities they're tasked with beyond just, well, catching and throwing the ball. By now you've probably heard about "framing" or the art of making umpires more likely to call balls outside the strike zone for strikes. To put this into one tidy number, we incorporate pitch tracking data (for the years it exists) and adjust for important factors like pitcher, umpire, batter, and home-field advantage using a mixed-model approach. This grants us a number for how many strikes the catcher is personally adding to (or subtracting from) his pitchers' performance ... which we then convert to runs added or lost using linear weights.

Framing is one of the biggest parts of determining catcher value, but we also take into account blocking balls from going past, whether a scorer deems it a passed ball or a wild pitch. We use a similar approach–one that really benefits from the pitch tracking data that tells us what ends up in the dirt and what doesn't. We also include a catcher's ability to prevent stolen bases and how well they field balls in play, and *finally* we come up with our FRAA for catchers.

Pitching

Both pitching and fielding make up the half of baseball that isn't run scoring: run prevention. Separating pitching from fielding is a tough task, and most recent pitching analysis has branched off from Voros McCracken's famous (and controversial) statement, "There is little if any difference among major-league pitchers in their ability to prevent hits on balls hit in the field of play." The research of the analytic community has validated this to some extent, and there are a host of "defense-independent" pitching measures that have been developed to try and extricate the effect of the defense behind a hurler from the pitcher's work.

Our solution to this quandry is Deserved Run Average (DRA), our core pitching metric. DRA looks like earned run average (ERA), the tried-and-true pitching stat you've seen on every baseball broadcast or box score from the past century, but it's very different. To start, DRA takes an event-by-event look at what the pitchers does, and adjusts the value of that event based on different environmental factors like park, batter, catcher, umpire, base-out situation, run differential, inning, defense, home field advantage, pitcher role, and temperature. That mixed model gives us a pitcher's expected contribution, similar to what we do for our DRC+ model for hitters and FRAA model for catchers. (Oh, and we also consider the pitcher's effect on basestealing and on balls getting past the catcher.)

It's important to note that DRA is set to the scale of runs allowed per nine innings (RA9) instead of ERA, which makes DRA's scale slightly higher than ERA's. The reason for this is because ERA tends to overrate three types of pitchers:

1. Pitchers who play in parks where scorers hand out more errors. Official scorers differ significantly in the frequency at which they assign errors to fielders.
2. Ground-ball pitchers, because a substantial proportion of errors occur on grounders.
3. Pitchers who aren't very good. Better pitchers often allow fewer unearned runs than bad pitchers, because good pitchers tend to find ways to get out of jams.

Since the last time you picked up an edition of this book, we've also made a few minor changes to DRA to make it better. Recent research into "tunneling"–the act of throwing consecutive pitches that appear similar from a batter's point of view until after the swing decision point–data has given us a new contextual factor to account for in DRA: plate distance. This refers to the distance between successive pitches as they approach the plate, and while it has a smaller effect than factors like velocity or whiff rate, it still can help explain pitcher strikeout rate in our model.

New Pitching Metrics for 2019

We're including a few "new" pitching metrics for 2019's suite of Baseball Prospectus publications, but you may be familiar with them if you've spent time scouring the internet for stats.

Fastball Percentage

Our fastball percentage (FB%) statistic measures how frequently a pitcher throws a pitch classified as a "fastball," measured as a percentage of overall pitches thrown. We qualify three types of fastballs:

1. The traditional four-seam fastball;
2. The two-seam fastball or sinker;
3. "Hard cutters," which are pitches that have the movement profile of a cut fastball and are used as the pitcher's primary offering or in place of a more traditional fastball.

For example, a pitcher with a FB% of 67 throws any combination of these three pitches about two-thirds of the time.

Whiff Rate

Everybody loves a swing and a miss, and whiff rate (WHF) measures how frequently pitchers induce a swinging strike. To calculate WHF, we add up all the pitches thrown that ended with a swinging strike, then divide that number by a pitcher's total pitches thrown. Most often, high whiff rates correlate with high strikeout rates (and overall effective pitcher performance).

Called Strike Probability

Called Strike Probability (CSP) is a number that represents the likelihood that all of a pitcher's pitches will be called a strike while controlling for location, pitcher and batter handedness, umpire and count. Here's how it works: on each pitch, our model determines how many times (out of 100) that a similar pitch was called for a strike given those factors mentioned above, and when normalized for each batter's strike zone. Then we average the CSP for all pitches thrown by a pitcher in a season, and that gives us the yearly CSP percentage you see in the stats boxes.

As you might imagine, pitchers with a higher CSP are more likely to work in the zone, where pitchers with a lower CSP are likely locating their pitches outside the normal strike zone, for better or for worse.

Projections

Many of you aren't turning to this book just for a look at what a player has done, but for a look at what a player is going to do: the PECOTA projections. PECOTA, initially developed by Nate Silver (who has moved on to greater fame as a political analyst), consists of three parts:

1. Major-league equivalencies, which use minor-league statistics to project how a player will perform in the major leagues;
2. Baseline forecasts, which use weighted averages and regression to the mean to estimate a player's current true talent level; and
3. Aging curves, which uses the career paths of comparable players to estimate how a player's statistics are likely to change over time.

With all those important things covered, let's take a look at what's in the book this year.

Team Prospectus

You bought this book to learn more about your favorite (or maybe least-favorite, who are we to judge?) team, so let's talk about them. After a thoughtful preview of the 2019 season, you'll be presented with our Team Prospectus. This outlines many of the key statistics for each team's 2018 season, as well as a very inviting stadium diagram.

First you'll find the Performance Graphs page. The first is the 2018 Hit List Ranking. This shows our Hit List Rank for the team on each day of the 2018 season and is intended to give you a picture of the ups and downs of the team's season, including their highest and lowest ranks of the year. Hit List Rank measures overall team performance and drives the Hit List Power Rankings at the baseballprospectus.com website.

The second graph is Committed Payroll and helps you see how the team's payroll has compared to the MLB and divisional average payrolls over time. Payroll figures are currents as of January 1, 2019; with so many free agents still unsigned as of this writing, the final 2018 figure will likely be significantly different for many teams. (In the meantime, you can always find the most current data at Baseball Prospectus' Cot's Baseball Contracts page.)

Houston Astros 2019

The third graph is Farm System Ranking and displays how the Baseball Prospectus prospect team has ranked the organization's farm system since 2007. It also indicates the highest and lowest ranks that the farm system achieved over that time.

We start the Team Performance page with the squad's unadjusted and third-order 2018 win-loss records, presented in divisional context. We then list the three highest performing hitters and pitchers by WARP for 2018. Beneath that are a host of other team statistics. **Pythag** presents an adjusted 2018 winning percentage, calculated by taking runs scored per game (**RS/G**) and runs allowed per game (**RA/G**) for the team, and running them through a version of Bill James' Pythagorean formula that was refined and improved by David Smyth and Brandon Heipp. (The formula is called "Pythagenpat," which is equally fun to type and to say.)

Next up is **DRC+**, described earlier, to indicate the overall hitting ability of the team either above or below league-average. Run prevention on the pitching side is covered by **DRA** (also mentioned earlier) and another metric: Fielding Independent Pitching (**FIP**), which calculates another ERA-like statistic based on strikeouts, walks, and home runs recorded. Defensive Efficiency Rating (**DER**) tells us the percentage of balls in play turned into outs for the team, and is a quick fielding shorthand that rounds out run prevention.

After that, we have several measures related to roster composition, as opposed to on-field performance. **B-Age** and **P-Age** tell us the average age of a team's batters and pitchers, respectively. **Salary** is the combined team payroll for all on-field players, and Doug Pappas' Marginal Dollars per Marginal Win (**M$/MW**) tells us how much money a team spent to earn production above replacement level.

Ending this batch of statistics is the number of disabled list days a team had over the season (**DL Days**) and the amount of salary paid to players on the disabled list (**$ on DL**); this final number is expressed as a percentage of total payroll.

Next to each of these stats, we've listed each team's MLB rank in that category from 1st to 30th. In this, 1st always indicates a positive outcome and 30th a negative outcome, except in the case of salary–1st is highest.

The Team Projections page is intended to convey the team's operational capacity entering the 2019 season. We start with the team's PECOTA projected record for 2019, again in divisional context. The **+/-** column indicates how many more or less wins the team is projected to get than they got in 2018. We then list the three highest projected hitters and pitchers by WARP for 2018. A brief farm system summary follows, with the team's top prospect and number of BP Top 101 Prospects. Finally, we list the key new players and departed players, along with their 2019 projected WARP.

Alex Bregman 3B

Born: 03/30/94 Age: 25 Bats: R Throws: R
Height: 6'0" Weight: 180 Origin: Round 1, 2015 Draft (#2 overall)

YEAR	TEAM	LVL	AGE	PA	R	2B	3B	HR	RBI	BB	K	SB	CS	AVG/OBP/SLG
2016	CCH	AA	22	285	54	16	2	14	46	42	26	5	3	.297/.415/.559
2016	FRE	AAA	22	83	17	6	0	6	15	5	12	2	1	.333/.373/.641
2016	HOU	MLB	22	217	31	13	3	8	34	15	52	2	0	.264/.313/.478
2017	HOU	MLB	23	626	88	39	5	19	71	55	97	17	5	.284/.352/.475
2018	HOU	MLB	24	705	105	51	1	31	103	96	85	10	4	.286/.394/.532
2019	HOU	MLB	25	675	96	38	3	23	78	73	107	12	4	.272/.359/.463

Breakout: 6% Improve: 52% Collapse: 5% Attrition: 2% MLB: 100%
Comparables: Anthony Rendon, David Wright, Pablo Sandoval

YEAR	TEAM	LVL	AGE	PA	DRC+	VORP	BABIP	BRR	FRAA	WARP
2016	CCH	AA	22	285	172	38.9	.286	1.6	SS(51): -3.4, 3B(11): 1.4	2.7
2016	FRE	AAA	22	83	161	10.0	.333	-1.2	SS(14): 2.1, LF(3): -0.1	0.8
2016	HOU	MLB	22	217	107	9.6	.317	0.5	3B(40): 0.9, SS(6): -0.1	1.1
2017	HOU	MLB	23	626	114	34.7	.311	-1.5	3B(132): 8.7, SS(30): -2.9	3.9
2018	HOU	MLB	24	705	150	72.6	.289	-1.6	3B(136): 5.4, SS(28): -0.4	7.4
2019	HOU	MLB	25	675	125	37.3	.295	0.0	3B 7, SS 0	4.6

After the projections page, we share a few items about the team's home ballpark. There's the aforementioned diagram of the park's dimensions (including distances to the outfield wall), a few important biographical facts about the stadium, a graphic showing the height of the wall from the left-field pole to the right-field pole, and a table showing three-year park factors for the stadium. The park factors are displayed as indexes where 100 is average, 110 means that the park inflates the statistic in question by 10 percent, and 90 means that the park deflates the statistic in question by 10 percent.

Following the ballpark page, we have a **Personnel** section that lists many of the important decision-makers and upper-level field and operations staff members for the franchise, as well as any former Baseball Prospectus staff members who are currently part of the organization.

Position Players

After all that information and a thoughtful bylined essay covering each team, we present our player comments. Each player is listed with the major-league team who employed him as of early January 2019. If a player changed teams after that point via free agency, trade, or any other method, you'll be able to find them in the book for their previous squad.

First, we cover biographical information (age is as of June 30, 2019) before moving onto the stats themselves. Our statistic columns include standard identifying information like **YEAR**, **TEAM**, **LVL** (level of affiliated play) and **AGE** before getting into the numbers. Next, we provide raw, unstranslated numbers like you might find on the back of your dad's baseball cards: **PA** (plate appearances), **R** (runs), **2B** (doubles), **3B** (triples), **HR** (home runs), **RBI** (runs batted in), **BB** (walks), **K** (strikeouts), **SB** (stolen bases) and **CS** (caught stealing). Then we have unadjusted "slash" statistics: **AVG** (batting average), **OBP** (on-base percentage) and **SLG** (slugging percentage).

Just below the stats box is **PECOTA** data, which is discussed further in a following section. After that, it's on to a pithy and always-informative comment written by a member of the Baseball Prospectus staff, before we cover more stats.

The second text box repeats YEAR, TEAM, LVL, AGE, and PA, then moves on to **DRC+** (Deserved Runs Created Plus), which we described earlier as total offensive expected contribution compared to the league average. Next, one of our oldest active metrics, **VORP** (Value Over Replacement Player), considers offensive production, position and plate appearances. In essence, it is the number of runs contributed beyond what a replacement-level player at the same position would contribute if given the same percentage of team plate appearances. VORP does not consider the quality of a player's defense.

BABIP (batting average on balls in play) tells us how often a ball in play fell for a hit, and can help us identify whether a batter may have been lucky or not … but note that high BABIPs also tend to follow the great hitters of our time, as well as speedy singles hitters who put the ball on the ground.

The next item is **BRR** (Baserunning Runs), which covers all of a player's baserunning accomplishments which includes (but isn't limited to) swiped bags and failed attempts. Next is **FRAA** (Fielding Runs Above Average), which also includes the number of games previously played at each position noted in parentheses. Multi-position players have only their two most frequent positions listed here, but their total FRAA number reflects all positions played.

Our last column here is **WARP** (Wins Above Replacement Player). WARP estimates the total value of a player, which means for hitters it takes into account hitting runs above average (calculated using the DRC+ model), BRR and FRAA. Then, it makes an adjustment for positions played and gives the player a credit for plate appearances based upon the difference between "replacement level"¬–which is derived from the quality of players added to a team's roster after the start of the season¬–and the league average.

Catchers

Catchers are a special breed, and thus they have earned their own separate box which displays some of the defensive metrics that we've built just for them. As an example, let's check out J.T. Realmuto.

YEAR	TEAM	P. COUNT	FRM RUNS	BLK RUNS	THRW RUNS	TOT RUNS
2016	MIA	18935	-8.5	1.8	2.1	-5.6
2017	MIA	18959	5.3	1.7	1.0	9.1
2018	MIA	16399	-0.4	0.9	0.1	0.4
2019	PHI	18448	-1.4	1.5	0.7	0.8

The **YEAR** and **TEAM** columns match what you'd find in the other stat box. **P. COUNT** indicates the number of pitches thrown while the catcher was behind the plate, including swinging strikes, fouls, and balls in play. **FRM RUNS** is the total run value the catcher provided (or cost) his team by influencing the umpire to call strikes where other catchers did not. **BLK RUNS** expresses the total run value above or below average for the catcher's ability to prevent wild pitches and passed balls. **THRW RUNS** is calculated using a similar model as the previous two statistics, and it measures a catcher's ability to throw out basestealers but also to dissuade them from testing his arm in the first place. It takes into account factors like the pitcher (including his delivery and pickoff move) and baserunner (who could be as fast as Billy Hamilton or as slow as Yonder Alonso). **TOT RUNS** is the sum of all of the previous three statistics.

Pitchers

Let's give our pitchers a turn, using 2018 NL Cy Young winner Jacob deGrom as our example. Take a look at his first stat block: the first line and the **YEAR**, **TEAM**, **LVL** and **AGE** columns are the same as in the position player example earlier.

Here too, we have a series of columns that display raw, unadjusted statistics compiled by the pitcher over the course of a season: **W** (wins), **L** (losses), **SV** (saves), **G** (games pitched), **GS** (games started), **IP** (innings pitched), **H** (hits allowed) and **HR** (home runs allowed). Next we have two statistics that are rates: **BB/9** (walks per nine innings) and **K/9** (strikeouts per nine innings), before returning to the unadjusted **K** (strikeouts).

Next up is **GB%** (ground ball percentage), which is the percentage of all batted balls that were hit in the ground, including both outs and hits. Remember, this is based on observational data and subject to human error, so please approach this with a healthy dose of skepticism.

BABIP (batting average on balls in play) is calculated using the same methodology as it is for position players, but it often tells us more about a pitcher than it does a hitter. With pitchers, a high BABIP is often due to poor defense or bad luck, and can often be an indicator of potential rebound, and a low BABIP may be cause to expect performance regression. (A typical league-average BABIP is close to .290-.300.)

After a witty 150ish words on the player like only Baseball Prospectus's staff can provide, it's on to that second stat block, which repeats the YEAR, TEAM, LVL, and AGE columns. The metrics **WHIP** (walks plus hits per inning pitched) and **ERA**

Houston Astros 2019

(earned run average) are old standbys: WHIP measures walks and hits allowed on a per-inning basis, while ERA measures earned runs on a nine-inning basis. Neither of these stats are translated or adjusted.

DRA (Deserved Run Average) was described at length earlier, and measures how many runs the pitcher "deserved" to allow per nine innings. Please note that since we lack all the data points that would make for a "real" DRA for minor-league events, the DRA displayed for minor league partial-seasons is based off of different data. (That data is a modified version of our cFIP metric, which you can find more information about on our website.)

Jacob deGrom   RHP
Born: 06/19/88   Age: 31   Bats: L   Throws: R
Height: 6'4"   Weight: 180   Origin: Round 9, 2010 Draft (#272 overall)

YEAR	TEAM	LVL	AGE	W	L	SV	G	GS	IP	H	HR	BB/9	K/9	K	GB%	BABIP
2016	NYN	MLB	28	7	8	0	24	24	148	142	15	2.2	8.7	143	47%	.312
2017	NYN	MLB	29	15	10	0	31	31	201¹	180	28	2.6	10.7	239	48%	.305
2018	NYN	MLB	30	10	9	0	32	32	217	152	10	1.9	11.2	269	48%	.281
2019	NYN	MLB	31	13	9	0	31	31	186	145	18	2.3	10.7	221	46%	.286

Breakout: 8%   Improve: 29%   Collapse: 28%   Attrition: 6%   MLB: 85%
Comparables: Erik Bedard, A.J. Burnett, CC Sabathia

YEAR	TEAM	LVL	AGE	WHIP	ERA	DRA	WARP	MPH	FB%	WHF	CSP
2016	NYN	MLB	28	1.20	3.04	3.30	3.5	96.3	59.6	12.1	47.2
2017	NYN	MLB	29	1.19	3.53	3.02	5.7	97.2	55.5	14.5	49.5
2018	NYN	MLB	30	0.91	1.70	2.09	8.0	98.2	52.1	16.3	48.4
2019	NYN	MLB	31	1.02	2.91	3.23	3.9	96.6	54.5	14.8	48.2

Just like with hitters, **WARP** (Wins Above Replacement Player) is a total value metric that puts pitchers of all stripes on the same scale as position players. We use DRA as the primary input for our calculation of WARP. You might notice that relief pitchers (due to their limited innings) may have a lower WARP than you were expecting or than you might see in other WARP-like metrics. WARP does not take leverage into account, just the actions a pitcher performs and the expected value of those actions ... which ends up judging high-leverage relief pitchers differently than you might imagine given their prestige and market value.

MPH gives you the pitcher's 95th percentile velocity for the noted season, in order to give you an idea of what the *peak* fastball velocity a pitcher possesses. Since this comes from our pitch tracking data, it is not publicly available for minor-league pitchers.

Finally, we display the three new pitching metrics we described earlier. **FB%** (fastball percentage) gives you the percentage of fastballs thrown out of all pitches. **WhiffRt** (whiff rate) tells you the percentage of swinging strikes induced out of all pitches. **CS Prob** (called strike probability) expresses the likelihood of all pitches thrown to result in a called strike, after controlling for factors like handedness, umpire, pitch type, count, and location.

PECOTA

All players have PECOTA projections for 2019, as well as a set of other numbers that describe the performance of comparable players according to PECOTA. All projections for 2019 are for the player at the date we went to press in early January and are projected into the league and park context as indicated by the team abbreviation. All PECOTA projected statistics represent a player's projected major-league performance.

The numbers beneath the player's stats–Breakout, Improve, Collapse, Attrition–are part and parcel of the PECOTA projections. They estimate the likelihood of changes in performance relative to the player's previously-established level of production, based on the performance of comparable players:

Breakout Rate is the percent change that a player's production will improve by at least 20 percent relative to the weighted average of his performance over his most recent seasons.

Improve Rate is the percent chance that a player's production will improve at all relative to his baseline performance. A player who is expected to perform just the same as he has in the recent past will have an Improve Rate of 50 percent.

Collapse Rate is the percent chance that a position player's production will decline by at least 25 percent relative to his baseline performance.

Attrition Rate operates on playing time rather than performance. Specifically, it measures the likelihood that a player's playing time will decrease by at least 50 percent relative to his established level.

Breakout Rate and Collapse Rate can sometimes be counterintuitive for players who have already experienced a radical change in performance level. It's also worth noting that the projected decline in a player's rate performances might not be indicative of an expected decline in underlying ability or skill, but could just be an anticipated correction following a breakout season.

MLB% is the percentage of similar players who played in the major leagues in their relevant season.

The final pieces of information are the player's three highest-scoring comparable players as determined by PECOTA. All comparables represent a snapshot of how the listed player was performing at the same age as the current player, so if a 23-year-old pitcher is compared to Bartolo Colon, he's actually being compared to a 23-year-old Colon, not the version that pitched for the Rangers in 2018, nor to Colon's career as a whole.

A few points about pitcher projections. First, we aren't yet projecting peak velocity, so that column will be blank in the PECOTA lines. Second, projecting DRA is trickier than evaluating past performance, because it is unclear how deserving each pitcher will be of his anticipated outcomes. However, we know that another DRA-related statistic–contextual FIP or cFIP–estimates future run scoring very well. So for PECOTA, the projected DRA figures you see are based on the past cFIPs generated by the pitcher and comparable players over time, along with the other factors described above.

Lineouts

In each chapter's Lineouts section, you'll find abbreviated text comments, as well as most of same information you'd find in our full player comments. We limit the stats boxes in this section to only including the 2018 information for each player.

Exclusive Player Visualizations

In our constant battle to provide you with new and interesting baseball content you can't find anywhere else, we've added a trio of data visualizations to each hitter's entry in these books and a pair of visualizations for each pitcher.

For hitters, you'll find three new infographics. The first is each player's **Batted Ball Distribution**, which displays the five major sections of the field: LF (left), LCF (left center), CF (center), RCF (right center), and RF (right). The percentage indicated tells us what percentage of batted balls from that hitter fell within that part of the field during the 2018 season. We've also included the hitter's slugging percentage on balls in play (also called **SLGCON**) for that part of the field.

You'll also see two heatmaps: **Strike Zone vs LHP** and **Strike Zone vs RHP**. These heat maps represent a view of the strike zone from behind the catcher. Areas where there is a darker coloration represent the places where a higher percentage of pitches resulted in hits. In other words, the heatmap represents a hitter's "sweet spots" for getting hits against either left-handed or right-handed pitchers, depending on the image.

Pitchers get two images that help explain what their pitches look like from a hitter's perspective: **Pitch Shape vs LHH** and **Pitch Shape vs RHH**. These images show you the shape and the "tunneling" effect of each pitcher's offerings from the batter's perspective. For each type of pitch that a pitcher throws (represented by an indicator shape), there's a set of dots indicating the flight path, where each dot represents a 0.01-second interval. This maps the average trajectory and speed of an offering, ending where the ball crosses the plate. The solid black box represents the regular strike zone, while the gray contour lines indicate the range of locations that a pitcher typically works in.

Below the image, we provide a bit more detailed information about each pitcher's average offering in the **Pitch Types** box. Here, we also list each of the pitcher's major offerings under the **Type** column.

- **Fastballs** (which usually refers to the four-seam variation)
- **Sinkers** and/or two-seam fastballs
- **Cutters** (which could include "hard" cutters like cut fastballs and "soft" cutters that resemble hard sliders)
- **Changeups** (not including most splitters)
- **Splitters** (split-fingered pitches, forkballs, and some split-changes)
- **Sliders** and/or slurves
- **Curveballs** (including spike-curveballs and knuckle-curveballs, as well as some slurvy curves)
- **Slow curveballs** and/or eephus pitches
- **Knuckleballs**
- **Screwballs**

The **Freq** column indicates the percentage of overall pitches that fall into each of those type categories; if a pitcher has a 16.55% score for changeups, then that's the percent of all pitches that he throws as changeups. **Velo** is exactly what you think it is: the average miles per hour for each pitch type. **H Mov** is the number of inches of horizontal movement on the average pitch of that type, while **V Mov** is the number of inches of vertical movement on the average pitch of that type. (At Baseball Prospectus, we measure this over the long flight of the ball and include gravity into the V Mov number in order to give you the most realistic representation of what the pitch *actually* does.)

If you're wondering about the second number in brackets, that's the index for that velocity or movement compared to the league average. Like DRC+, a score of 100 means that the speed or movement is about the same as league average, while a higher score means that there's higher velocity or movement than the league average. Numbers below 100 indicate less velocity or movement than the league average.

Part 1: Team Analysis

Table for Two: Previewing the 2019 Houston Astros

Wilson Karaman and Rob Mains

ROB MAINS: It's pretty hard for me to see the Astros not winning their division again. On the other hand, I don't know that they've improved themselves much. I like Michael Brantley, but I don't see Wade Miley as the equal of the departed Dallas Keuchel and Charlie Morton, and Aledmys Diaz is sort of poor man's Marwin Gonzalez, right? Was the offseason approach to throw a little spackle over the holes and assume that Josh James, Forrest Whitley, Tyler White, and Kyle Tucker are ready to step up?

WILSON KARAMAN: It's a dope position, right? Last year they could very well have had a higher ceiling than the title team that preceded them, and yet they never really felt fully healthy and whole. I think what you say is right, insofar as the math theory here is that you effectively have to replace about eight WARP that walked out the door in order to break even. Well, Brantley, Miley, and Chirinos (don't forget him!) might only get you halfway there. But then you had a situation last year where Correa, Altuve, and Springer combined to give you "only" a hair under nine. If you're expecting 13, 14, 15 from them this year instead… plus you've got all that young talent you mentioned… it's still a catbird seat, and a comfy one at that.

Speaking of that young talent, who ya got as far as which one of those guys steps up the most and proves most valuable in the team's effort to "take it back"?

ROB: I always overlook Chirinos because he's only about three months younger than Brian McCann. Literally.

The Derek Fisher Experience has probably made me irrationally cautious about Tucker, and Brantley makes that outfield crowded. So among the rookie crop, I like the outlook for Forrest Whitley, and not just because we rank him as the No. 7 prospect overall. The Astros have a place for him, and the depth to bring him on slowly. Houston seems to be doing right in their pitcher development; who saw James coming on like he did? Are you a Whitley guy?

WILSON: The Josh James sleep apnea revolution is one of the better stories the game put forth last season. When I saw him at Lancaster at the beginning of 2016 I put an NP (non-prospect) grade on him with this write-up: "FB 88-90, will cut it, poor location, elevating and leaking; uphill motion, short/quick leg kick, balance issues, some crossfire; 81-82 SL flashes some bite, very inconsistent." Dude sat 98 and generated one of the five best whiff-per-swing rates in the world with his slider after he hit the bigs last year. Even found a workable third pitch. Incredible.

It's pretty hard *not* to be a Whitley guy. He's a 6-foot-7 monster who commands five pitches as well as anybody with that much length and size. He's so good that he threw what, 25 innings all of last year and *still* emerged as the more-or-less undisputed Best Pitching Prospect in Baseball. Also incredible.

I'm going to tip the scale narrowly in James' favor as my pick to produce the most value out of that quartet for the 2019 Astros. He's tailor-made for their pitching staff philosophy in a McCullers kind of role, and lest we forget, that position is vacant. Note that I also buy Tyler White's hitting ability. While PECOTA is only modestly supportive of this theory (112 projected DRC+), I think he's absolutely capable of taking that DH role and running with it.

Speaking of PECOTA, we've now seen veterans Justin Verlander and Gerrit Cole both come over in the last couple years and morph (or in Verlander's case re-morph) into six-plus WARP pitchers. Charlie Morton became a three-win guy. Enter Wade Miley. Does Houston know something everyone else—including PECOTA, it of the 0.5 WARP projection—doesn't?

ROB: Well, the Brewers were able to squeeze a 2.57 ERA out of 80 2/3 innings last year, and while the peripherals (5.6 K/9!) didn't completely support it, his 3.55 FIP and 4.13 DRA were better than league average. I could see the Astros picking his spots sufficiently to get something like a high-3s ERA out of him, but a repeat of 2018 would be unnatural. We're not talking about a Verlander-like return to prior form.

I was thinking about the Astros rotation. Last season, the Astros used only five starting pitchers (Verlander, Keuchel, Cole, Morton, and Lance McCullers) from Opening Day through August 20. Betcha they don't do that again! Is this the year Verlander finally acts his age? (Or, for that matter, Miley's 32.) Gurriel turns 35 in June. Reddick's 32. Who collapses on this team? We're projecting a below-average 99 DRC+ for Gurriel this year, which really doesn't work for a corner guy. Who's your collapse candidate?

WILSON: Whiffing less than six guys per nine these days is a truly Herculean accomplishment, yeah. The thing about Verlander is that he has left nary a breadcrumb that he's on the verge of any kind of a collapse. And what's cool about him is that not only has he held (or, re-discovered and maintained, I guess?) his impact velo for so much longer than most frontline starters, he's gotten even *more* fastball-centric since moving to Houston. It's been an open defiance. Guy's a no-doubt Hall of Famer, and no-doubt Hall of Famers are capable of magical things.

Gurriel's the guy PECOTA is betting against as well, but if I had to look for a sneaky candidate it might be Springer? He's shed a consistent .3 to .4 miles-an-hour of sprint speed annually for the last four years running now and posted his first negative FRAA season last year. The groundball rate nudged up, and the quality and consistency of contact down. He's also run into a bunch of walls, jostled his shoulders on catch attempts, and on down the list of minor maladies over years of playing max-effort ball. Last year's dents were the most recent in a long string of minor knocks that pile up on bodies as they head into the 30 turn. I dunno, no blaring reggaeton horns or anything, and he yet again destroyed all comers in October. But there are just enough sum-of-parts things starting to creep in to make me mildly skeptical of him bouncing all the way back into five-WARP range.

The thing I come back to is that this feels like an important year for everything to go right for this club. They'll again enter the year as one of the most talented teams in the game. But this year'll be Year Three of what, through the course of their drafting, development, and spending/acquisition strategy, may just be a three-year window of championship-caliber contending. Verlander, Cole, McHugh, and the vast majority of relief pitchers without a known record of domestic abuse can walk after the season. Altuve's salary escalation kicks in and jumps him $29 million annually starting next year. Bregman hits arbitration, Correa and Springer get more expensive moving through that process… what say you, do you sense a potential shift change on the horizon? Where do you see these Astros going over the medium-term?

ROB: Well, I think they first thank their lucky stars that they play in a division with a team that doesn't understand the concept of sunk money, a team whose owner refuses to pony up for top-tier talent, and two teams that are legitimately in rebuild mode. But for Houston to stay relevant for the next few years I think two things will have to happen. First, the farm system is going to have to continue to produce. (The Astros have four of the game's top 50 prospects, so this is not a stretch.) Second–and we have no visibility into this–Jim Crane, with a reported net worth of $2 billion, is going to have to part with some of those dollars in order to retain and/or attract talent.

Houston ended last season with the seventh-most-expensive 40-man roster in baseball at $187.4 million but over $50 million of that is no longer with the club. My guess is that they mostly keep the band together. Maybe not Springer, who'll be 31 when he can file for free agency, leaving aside your legitimate concerns about his performance as he ages. I have a hard time seeing them claiming they "can't afford" a healthy Correa or Bregman or Cole, but I think there's a risk that they go full Cleveland, trying to titrate the absolute smallest payroll outlay that will get them into October. The problem with that approach, obviously, is that sometimes you guess wrong and you're watching the A's pour alcoholic beverages over one another's heads.

But for the next couple years, at least, this club strikes me as too talented, and the rest of the division too flawed to challenge them for the divisional crown. Do you see a realistic scenario that doesn't involve Houston in the postseason?

WILSON: No. No, I do not. I mean, I'll caveat that with the requisite eternal caveat: anything can happen across six months. Oakland's got one of the deeper 25U cores going, and the Orange County Trouts of Anaheim can hang around. But Houston remains a smart, resourceful, innovative, and deeply talented franchise on and off the field, with a credible case as the best Major League Baseball has to offer right now. They're the Champs once removed, and they look as poised as they could hope to go crown huntin' again.

PECOTA has them as the only team in baseball to win 98 games. You agree they'll win more games than anyone else? You taking the over or the under?

ROB: I'm gonna take the under, but with an asterisk. The morning of July 25 last year, Houston had a 67-36 record, a .650 winning percentage (.700 Pythagorean) and a six-game lead over the fading Mariners. From that point forward, their winning percentage was 40 points lower even though they finished the season playing their last 19 games against the playing-out-the-string (at best) Tigers, Diamondbacks, Mariners, Angels, Blue Jays, and Orioles. At the exact same point in 2017, they'd won two-thirds of their games, had an 11.5 game lead, and they played .556 ball the rest of the way.

They're like a 10K runner with a big lead who looks back during the final lap and eases up to the finish. The goal isn't to bludgeon the AL West into submission (though PECOTA has them winning by 18 games!) but to get everybody rested for a deep run into October. So I say they fall short of 98, but by choice. Of PECOTA's three scary monsters in the AL, it sees Houston as the best balanced–better offense than Cleveland, better run prevention than New York–which sounds right to me. But I could see Boston pushing the Yankees to a stronger final lap and maybe a win or two more. How's that sound?

WILSON: That sounds like a wrap to me!

Performance Graphs

2018 Hit List Ranking

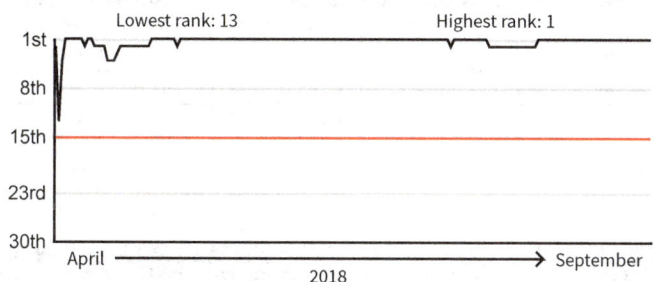

Committed Payroll (in millions)

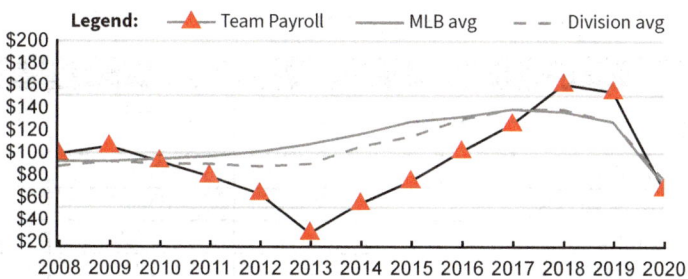

Farm System Ranking

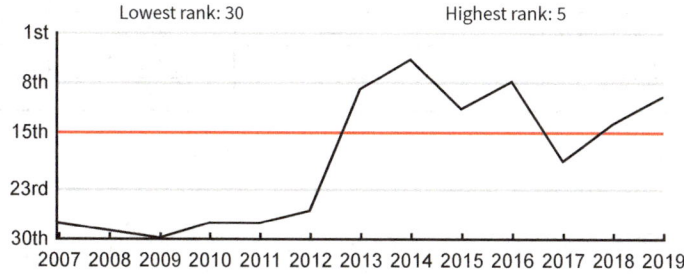

2018 Team Performance

ACTUAL STANDINGS

Team	W	L	Pct
HOU	**103**	**59**	**.635**
OAK	97	65	.598
SEA	89	73	.549
ANA	80	82	.493
TEX	67	95	.413

THIRD-ORDER STANDINGS

Team	W	L	Pct
HOU	**108**	**54**	**.666**
OAK	96	66	.592
SEA	82	80	.506
ANA	80	82	.493
TEX	68	94	.419

TOP HITTERS

Player	WARP
Alex Bregman	7.4
Jose Altuve	3.2
George Springer	2.9

TOP PITCHERS

Player	WARP
Justin Verlander	7.3
Gerrit Cole	6.4
Charlie Morton	3.1

VITAL STATISTICS

Statistic Name	Value	Rank
Pythagenpat	.675	1st
Runs Scored per Game	4.92	6th
Runs Allowed per Game	3.30	1st
Deserved Runs Created Plus	109	3rd
Deserved Run Average	3.15	1st
Fielding Independent Pitching	3.26	1st
Defensive Efficiency Rating	.717	5th
Batter Age	28.1	17th
Pitcher Age	30.0	27th
Salary	$160.4M	9th
Marginal $ per Marginal Win	$2.7M	24th
Disabled List Days	$859.0M	5th
$ on DL	7%	1st

2019 Team Projections

PROJECTED STANDINGS

Team	W	L	Pct	+/-
HOU	**98**	**64**	**.604**	**-5**
ANA	80	82	.493	0
OAK	79	83	.487	-18
TEX	71	91	.438	+4
SEA	70	92	.432	-19

TOP PROJECTED HITTERS

Player	WARP
Alex Bregman	4.6
Jose Altuve	4.5
Carlos Correa	4.0

TOP PROJECTED PITCHERS

Player	WARP
Gerrit Cole	4.0
Justin Verlander	3.6
Josh James	2.6

FARM SYSTEM REPORT

Top Prospect	Number of Top 101 Prospects
Forrest Whitley, #7	5

KEY DEDUCTIONS

Player	WARP
Martin Maldonado	4
Charlie Morton	2.7
Marwin Gonzalez	1.6
J.D. Davis	1.4
Brian McCann	0.9

KEY ADDITIONS

Player	WARP
Michael Brantley	1.4
Aledmys Diaz	0.8
Wade Miley	0.6
Robinson Chirinos	0.6

Team Personnel

General Manager
Jeff Luhnow

Assistant General Manager
Brandon Taubman

Special Assistant, Player Personnel
Kevin Goldstein

Special Assistant, Baseball Operations
Oz Ocampo

Manager
A.J. Hinch

BP Alumni
Kevin Goldstein
Colin Wyers

Minute Maid Park Stats

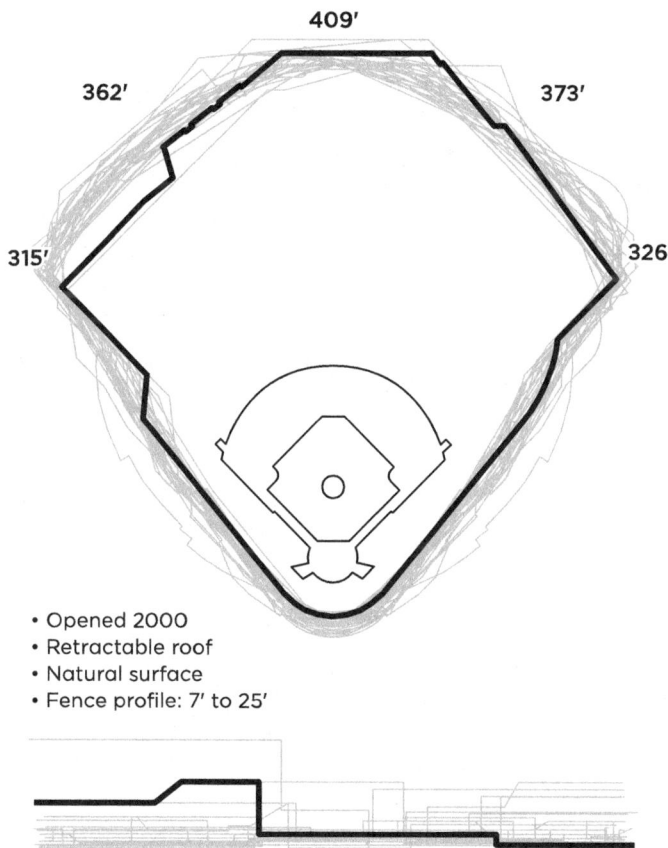

- Opened 2000
- Retractable roof
- Natural surface
- Fence profile: 7' to 25'

Three-Year Park Factors

Runs	Runs/RH	Runs/LH	HR/RH	HR/LH
94	94	95	101	96

Astros Team Analysis

In the seventh game of the 2017 American League Championship Series against the New York Yankees, Alex Bregman made a perfect play. With one out in the fifth inning, Todd Frazier was at the plate, Greg Bird was 90 feet from home, and Bregman—then a salty and accomplished young player whose excellence was dimmed a bit by the brilliance of teammates Jose Altuve and Carlos Correa, now a salty and accomplished young MVP candidate—was offscreen, patrolling third. You can well enough imagine what he looked like before the pitch: a forward lean, a stare suggestive of distaste with all those moments in a game that don't directly involve him. Frazier hit a bouncer to shallow third and Bird took off. In one motion—weirdly slow-seeming even before the slo-mo replays that followed—Bregman collected the ball at his stomach and snapped it to Brian McCann at the plate. The throw had the trajectory of a landing plane, all downsloping speed, no gravitational slack. It got to McCann's glove an inch off the dirt, a foot in front of the plate, an instant before Bird's cleat.

The play was perfect in design, in timing and in all three dimensions: equal parts instinct and technique. Maybe the most pleasing part of its perfection, though, was that it wasn't at all rare, in the context of that Houston team. Those Astros—with a 101-win regular season behind them and a World Series championship en route—were the most refreshing kind of juggernaut, one whose quality didn't depend on predictability. They were the sport's daily best bet to show you something you hadn't seen before. Altuve hit his 39 doubles 39 different ways; Correa cast his bat out and pulled it in along every axis. Their lineup had the depth of an overstocked Yankee squad with none of the drudgery; their pitching staff featured Dallas Keuchel's foggy inventory and, by the end of the year, Justin Verlander's high heat. They stretched rallies and walloped homers and struck out sides and choreographed impromptu infield ballets, painting over their own not-yet-dry bits of impossibility. Bregman's fifth-inning geometry didn't even end up being The Thing from that ALCS closer; Lance McCullers came out of the bullpen to throw four innings of one-hit relief, finishing it off with 24 consecutive curveballs.

I don't know why, then, Bregman's play is the one I think of when I think of the consistent newnesses the pre-championship Astros were made up of—or, more to the point, why it's the one I miss when I watch them now.

Houston Astros 2019

⚾   ⚾   ⚾

There's a small but crucial difference between trying to do something and trying to do it again. The 2018 Astros were a testament to this difference. They spent the offseason between title and title defense seemingly becoming only more themselves—adding Gerrit Cole's G-forces to their spin-rate-laden pitching staff last January, bringing back every offensive contributor of note, settling in for what looked like (what still looks like) a half-decade of comfortable contention. "That's been our goal all along," Houston general manager Jeff Luhnow said at the time of the Cole trade, "to get to the point of competitiveness and win a championship and hopefully win multiple championships."

But the GM-speak sterility in the above quote—the '17 Astros had gotten "to the point of competitiveness" in the way that Debussy "approached a viable melody"—seemed to manifest, at times, on the field. It's not that last season's Astros weren't excellent. They won two more regular-season games than the year before and rolled over the Cleveland Indians in the division series, the rotation missed bats and singed eyebrows, and the lineup piled up 797 runs against just 534 allowed. It's that, broadly, they seemed more dutiful in their approach. The sense of discovery that shot through the championship team gave way to one of recitation, of formulas followed and expected outcomes realized.

This is by far the preferable of the common trajectories for defending champions, of course, the other being a drowsy year-after letdown. And the Astros had some good excuses for being a little less fun: Altuve, Correa, and George Springer missed a combined 99 games. The greater source of displeasure, though, lay counterintuitively in just how well everything else *worked*. Verlander continued his late-career renaissance, putting up a 2.52 ERA over 34 starts, and Cole panned out spectacularly, with a 2.88 mark. Charlie Morton chipped in with the latest in a string of career years. The offense had enough margin for error to make up for the injuries to its stars and the regressions of nearly every major contributor. The illogical causation feels true: the Astros lost some of their magic because they didn't need it.

Back in 2017, the main drawback to that Houston team—that it was assembled via one of the more anti-competitive and cost-cutting spells of tanking in recent MLB history, that it marked a clear victory for the model of efficiency that now has even competitive teams selling off mid-career stars—was easy to ignore in favor of the plain lovability of the squad itself. Who could think of incentivized cynicism when Altuve and Correa were turning a double play, or when Marwin Gonzalez was slicing singles and filling in everywhere, or when Springer made the World Series the setting for the world's most indulgent physics experiment? Even if the template was legible, with all those ill-gotten high picks turning into world-beaters right on schedule, the specifics were thrillingly non-formulaic.

Now, organizational shrewdness is the Astros' story. Idiosyncrasy remains—Altuve's somehow predictive swing, the apple-in-an-earthquake action of Verlander's breaking ball—but it is all folded into the perfection of the larger design. That Houston's 2017 title required feats as extreme as Altuve's MVP and Springer's Series breakout seems incongruous, in retrospect; this is a team that no longer needs anything out of the ordinary to happen in order to win.

⚾ ⚾ ⚾

So, Bregman. It is an odd thing to complain about a player's improvement, especially when the result is a Gold Glove-caliber infielder who slashes .286/.394/.532 with 31 homers, a league-leading 51 doubles, and more walks than strikeouts. But Bregman's transition from a figure of partially-realized potential to a source of clockwork line-drive-walloping dovetails in a not wholly pleasant way with the Astros' growth from baseball's upstarts to one of its constants.

The present Bregman is a nearly faultless player: quick glove, strong arm, clipped but potent swing, rapt attention. He hits homers and snares liners and studies Spanish to make for easier on-field communication. He's due for a pay increase when he becomes arbitration-eligible next year and a much more substantial one when he reaches free agency in 2023, but for now, he's as valuable an asset as any in the game. "He is baseball," his manager says.

It might be more accurate to say that he is the Houston Astros. His inefficiencies, like those of the organization, have been sanded away. His approach is not bland, but neither is it quite as fresh—as reliably surprising, in that old Astro way—as it used to be. In some ways, back in '17, Bregman seemed to stand in for the team as a whole even more than Altuve or Correa or Springer or Verlander. He was the youngest of the young stars and the least-known of the figures getting introduced to national audiences, the avatar of a precociousness that hadn't yet given way to unqualified, title-officialized greatness. He was still a revelation, maybe in a way that only players who haven't yet lifted the Commissioner's Trophy and received MVP votes can be.

That throw in Game 7 against the Yankees summed it up. The play was superb, like the Astros were and are, but it was also reckless. It was made by a 23-year-old still shouldering his way up the pecking order, on behalf of a team trying to win the title in front of them, not position itself for one or two more. It was a desperate play, in the finest sense of the word; it set aside caution to try for something perfect.

But the era of invention in Houston, and its assault on our reason, is complete. Originals come from the windblind fury of creation, sequels from care and management. Now, the Astros are doing what they were always supposed to do, what their architects drew up. A team designed for the long haul is settling into its purpose. Houston will rack up 100 wins again, or close to it, and play important games in October, and maybe win another championship. Altuve or Correa or Bregman might win an MVP; Verlander or Cole might win a Cy Young.

This is, of course, an enviable position. It is what teams and players alike work for—to turn fleeting success into something lasting, to find and then replicate lightning in a bottle. Baseball especially encourages its participants towards steadiness; its daily demands render that '17 kind of magic untenable, eventually. It is Bregman's job to become so good that he doesn't need to be so daring; it is the front office's job to assemble a roster complete enough that it doesn't need an iconic hitting season to pace it. The Astros are as close a thing as MLB has to an ideal team, and they figure to be so for some time. They're just a little different—a little more certain, a little less fun—than when they weren't quite there.

—Robert O'Connell is a freelance sportswriter whose work has appeared in The Athletic and Deadspin.

Part 2: Player Analysis

Jose Altuve 2B

Born: 05/06/90   Age: 29   Bats: R   Throws: R
Height: 5'6"   Weight: 165   Origin: International Free Agent, 2007

YEAR	TEAM	LVL	AGE	PA	R	2B	3B	HR	RBI	BB	K	SB	CS	AVG/OBP/SLG
2016	HOU	MLB	26	717	108	42	5	24	96	60	70	30	10	.338/.396/.531
2017	HOU	MLB	27	662	112	39	4	24	81	58	84	32	6	.346/.410/.547
2018	HOU	MLB	28	599	84	29	2	13	61	55	79	17	4	.316/.386/.451
2019	HOU	MLB	29	627	85	32	3	17	76	64	81	25	7	.308/.386/.470

Breakout: 0%   Improve: 34%   Collapse: 10%   Attrition: 4%   MLB: 99%
Comparables: Dustin Pedroia, Roberto Alomar, Frankie Frisch

Despite a multitude of evidence to the contrary, it would appear that Altuve is, indeed, a human being. And human beings need at least two functioning knees to properly play the game of baseball. After fouling a pitch off his foot in April and stealing a single base all month, Altuve jammed one of his two human knees in July and his second half suffered for it. Of course, because he's Jose Altuve, he still performed a good deal above replacement level, but he certainly wasn't healthy enough to repeat his MVP numbers from the year prior. He should be ready to go come spring, and barring freak injury, the main question about his long-term future will be whether the power will rebound enough to offset his slowly-rising swinging strike percentage. He's Altuve, though. He's probably fine.

YEAR	TEAM	LVL	AGE	PA	DRC+	VORP	BABIP	BRR	FRAA	WARP
2016	HOU	MLB	26	717	148	66.3	.347	3.2	2B(148): -7.2, SS(1): 0.0	5.9
2017	HOU	MLB	27	662	140	64.1	.370	2.7	2B(149): -0.1	5.6
2018	HOU	MLB	28	599	126	41.9	.352	2.4	2B(130): -7.9	3.2
2019	HOU	MLB	29	627	137	52.2	.335	2.1	2B -7	4.5

Jose Altuve, continued

Batted Ball Distribution

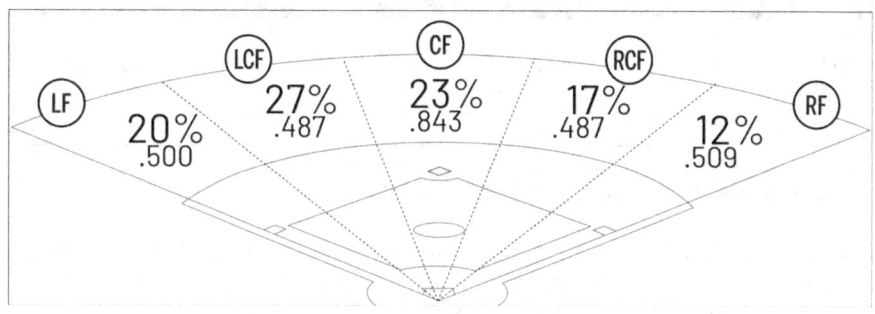

Strike Zone vs LHP

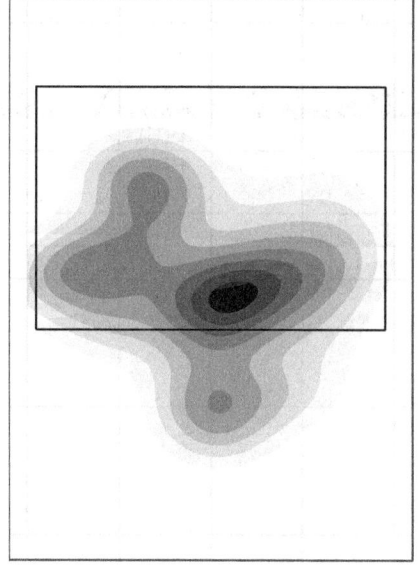

Strike Zone vs RHP

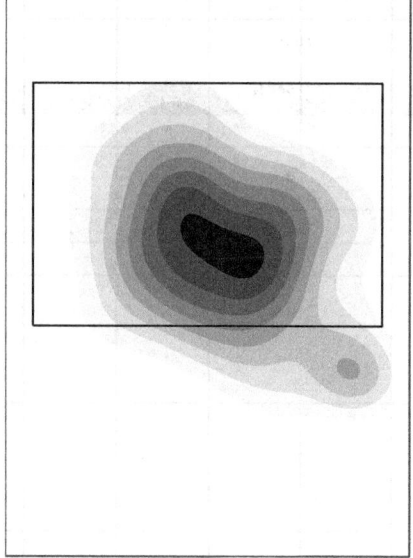

Michael Brantley LF

Born: 05/15/87   Age: 32   Bats: L   Throws: L
Height: 6'2"   Weight: 200   Origin: Round 7, 2005 Draft (#205 overall)

YEAR	TEAM	LVL	AGE	PA	R	2B	3B	HR	RBI	BB	K	SB	CS	AVG/OBP/SLG
2016	CLE	MLB	29	43	5	2	0	0	7	3	6	1	0	.231/.279/.282
2017	CLE	MLB	30	375	47	20	1	9	52	31	50	11	1	.299/.357/.444
2018	CLE	MLB	31	631	89	36	2	17	76	48	60	12	3	.309/.364/.468
2019	HOU	MLB	32	502	57	25	2	11	55	41	80	10	2	.272/.335/.408

Breakout: 1%   Improve: 36%   Collapse: 12%   Attrition: 10%   MLB: 98%
Comparables: Melky Cabrera, Tony Gwynn, Shannon Stewart

Brantley cleared 600 plate appearances for the first time since 2014 and showed he might have a good amount left in the tank after all, pulling his strikeout rate back down after seeing it inflate in his two previous injury-shortened seasons. The result was a classic prime Brantley season chock full of contact and just enough power to keep pitchers honest. One of the all-time great players to be named later, Brantley turns 32 in May, but 2018 represented a serious reversal of some disturbing trends, and a welcome return to form for a fun, unusual player in the current era.

YEAR	TEAM	LVL	AGE	PA	DRC+	VORP	BABIP	BRR	FRAA	WARP
2016	CLE	MLB	29	43	87	-1.0	.265	0.4	LF(11): 0.3	0.1
2017	CLE	MLB	30	375	106	13.7	.325	-0.6	LF(87): 5.2	1.7
2018	CLE	MLB	31	631	118	31.8	.319	1.4	LF(134): -3.4	2.8
2019	HOU	MLB	32	502	103	13.8	.309	0.8	LF 0	1.4

Michael Brantley, continued

Batted Ball Distribution

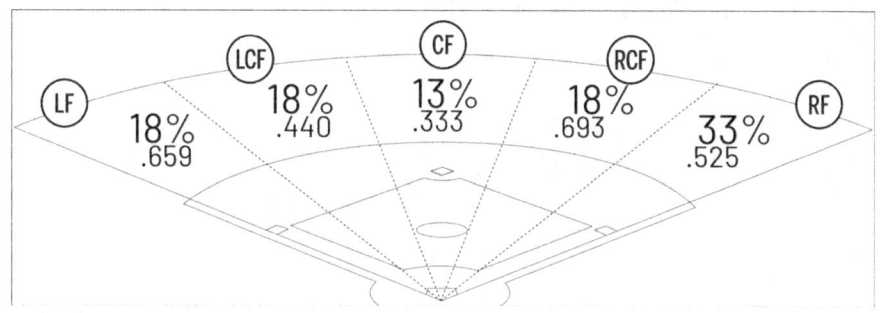

Strike Zone vs LHP

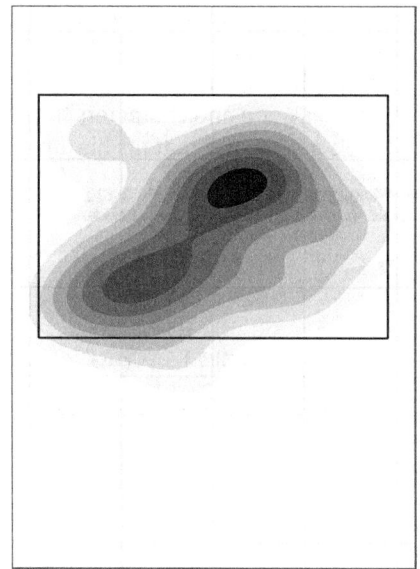

Strike Zone vs RHP

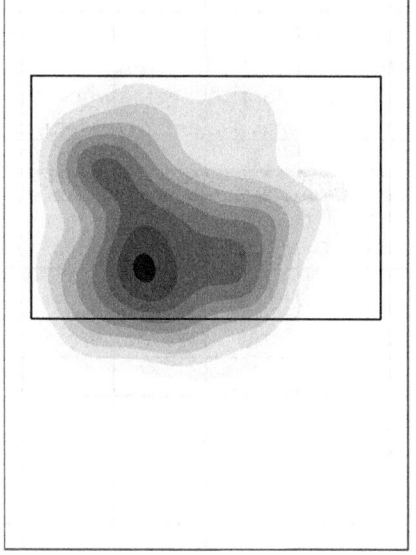

Alex Bregman 3B

Born: 03/30/94   Age: 25   Bats: R   Throws: R
Height: 6'0"   Weight: 180   Origin: Round 1, 2015 Draft (#2 overall)

YEAR	TEAM	LVL	AGE	PA	R	2B	3B	HR	RBI	BB	K	SB	CS	AVG/OBP/SLG
2016	CCH	AA	22	285	54	16	2	14	46	42	26	5	3	.297/.415/.559
2016	FRE	AAA	22	83	17	6	0	6	15	5	12	2	1	.333/.373/.641
2016	HOU	MLB	22	217	31	13	3	8	34	15	52	2	0	.264/.313/.478
2017	HOU	MLB	23	626	88	39	5	19	71	55	97	17	5	.284/.352/.475
2018	HOU	MLB	24	705	105	51	1	31	103	96	85	10	4	.286/.394/.532
2019	HOU	MLB	25	675	96	38	3	23	78	73	107	12	4	.272/.359/.463

Breakout: 6%   Improve: 52%   Collapse: 5%   Attrition: 2%   MLB: 100%
Comparables: Anthony Rendon, David Wright, Pablo Sandoval

The total package: He hits for average. He hits for power. He walks more than he strikes out. He plays a sterling third base. He's versatile enough to play the middle infield when Correa or Altuve isn't around. He hustles like a madman. He's funny on social media. He dunks on Trevor "Tyler" Bauer. He's one of the best interviews in the game. He's socially conscious. He's not exactly perfect as a player or a personality—I suppose he could run a little better, although he's certainly not slow, and sometimes his antics cross the imaginary line. But baseball is a far richer game when it has players this good and characters this fun. Bregman is a talent for any era, but also, he's a superstar that fits his time.

YEAR	TEAM	LVL	AGE	PA	DRC+	VORP	BABIP	BRR	FRAA	WARP
2016	CCH	AA	22	285	172	38.9	.286	1.6	SS(51): -3.4, 3B(11): 1.4	2.7
2016	FRE	AAA	22	83	161	10.0	.333	-1.2	SS(14): 2.1, LF(3): -0.1	0.8
2016	HOU	MLB	22	217	107	9.6	.317	0.5	3B(40): 0.9, SS(6): -0.1	1.1
2017	HOU	MLB	23	626	114	34.7	.311	-1.5	3B(132): 8.7, SS(30): -2.9	3.9
2018	HOU	MLB	24	705	150	72.6	.289	-1.6	3B(136): 5.4, SS(28): -0.4	7.4
2019	HOU	MLB	25	675	125	37.3	.295	0.0	3B 7, SS 0	4.6

Alex Bregman, continued

Batted Ball Distribution

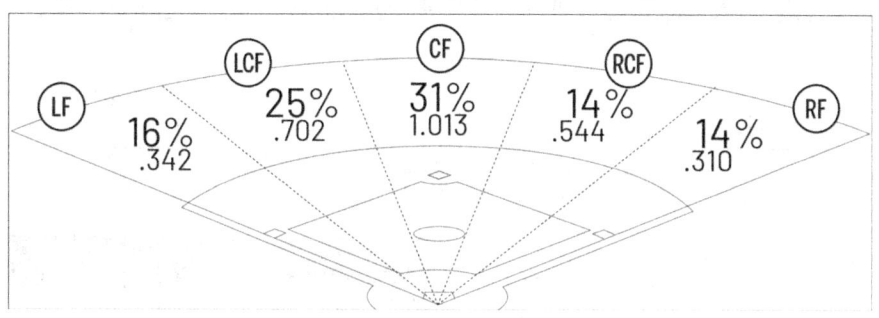

Strike Zone vs LHP   **Strike Zone vs RHP**

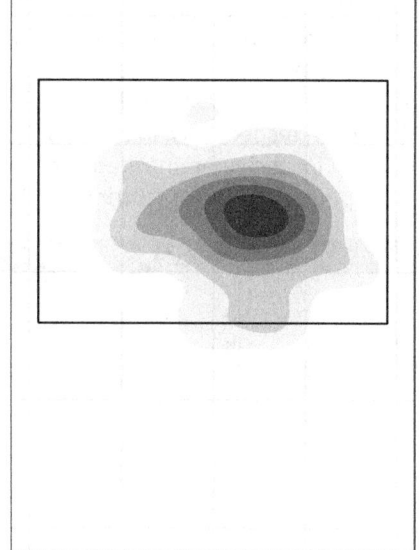

Robinson Chirinos C

Born: 06/05/84   Age: 35   Bats: R   Throws: R
Height: 6'1"   Weight: 210   Origin: International Free Agent, 2000

YEAR	TEAM	LVL	AGE	PA	R	2B	3B	HR	RBI	BB	K	SB	CS	AVG/OBP/SLG
2016	TEX	MLB	32	170	21	11	0	9	20	15	44	0	1	.224/.314/.483
2017	TEX	MLB	33	309	46	13	1	17	38	34	79	1	0	.255/.360/.506
2018	TEX	MLB	34	426	48	15	1	18	65	45	140	2	0	.222/.338/.419
2019	HOU	MLB	35	330	40	14	1	12	40	32	92	1	0	.236/.332/.419

Breakout: 0%   Improve: 27%   Collapse: 27%   Attrition: 16%   MLB: 88%
Comparables: Doug Mirabelli, Jason Varitek, David Ross

Chirinos caught more than 100 games in a season for the first time in 2018. That's great news for a well-loved clubhouse favorite who has battled concussions and other injuries for most of his career. The downside is that he threw out just 10 percent of

YEAR	TEAM	P. COUNT	FRM RUNS	BLK RUNS	THRW RUNS	TOT RUNS
2016	TEX	6797	-7.4	1.9	0.0	-6.5
2017	TEX	11679	-1.6	2.4	-0.9	0.2
2018	TEX	15072	-11.2	0.7	-0.8	-11.0
2019	HOU	12609	-8.7	1.7	-1.1	-8.1

runners attempting to steal, which is more commensurate with a teenage employee at Michael's craft store than it is a big-league catcher (league average in 2018 was 28 percent). Perhaps it was a one-off: Chirinos threw out 29, 27 and 25 percent, respectively, in 2015-2017. Or perhaps the greater workload was a bit much for the veteran. Whatever the case, Texas decided not to exercise their 2019 option on Chirinos, cutting him loose in favor of defensive guru Jeff Mathis.

YEAR	TEAM	LVL	AGE	PA	DRC+	VORP	BABIP	BRR	FRAA	WARP
2016	TEX	MLB	32	170	97	9.1	.250	0.2	C(54): -5.2	0.2
2017	TEX	MLB	33	309	121	20.8	.298	-1.7	C(85): -0.2	2.2
2018	TEX	MLB	34	426	107	22.0	.304	-1.4	C(108): -10.8	1.2
2019	HOU	MLB	35	330	104	16.7	.295	-0.5	C -9	0.6

Robinson Chirinos, continued

Batted Ball Distribution

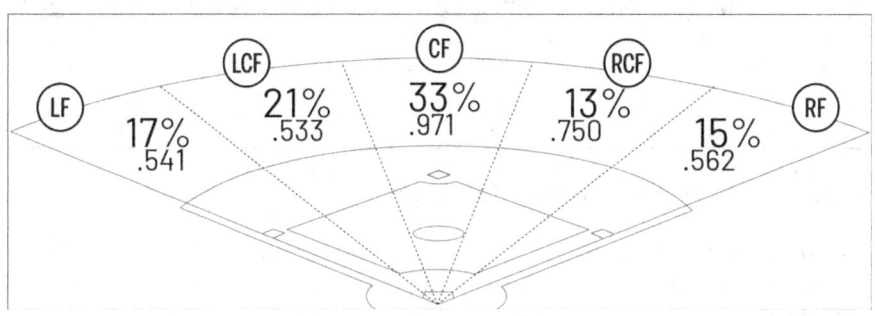

Strike Zone vs LHP   **Strike Zone vs RHP**

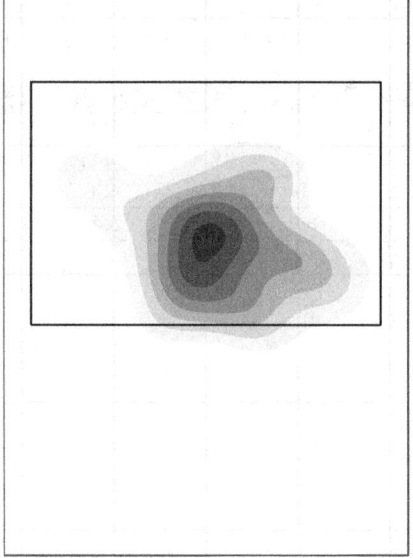

Carlos Correa SS

Born: 09/22/94   Age: 24   Bats: R   Throws: R
Height: 6'4"   Weight: 215   Origin: Round 1, 2012 Draft (#1 overall)

YEAR	TEAM	LVL	AGE	PA	R	2B	3B	HR	RBI	BB	K	SB	CS	AVG/OBP/SLG
2016	HOU	MLB	21	660	76	36	3	20	96	75	139	13	3	.274/.361/.451
2017	HOU	MLB	22	481	82	25	1	24	84	53	92	2	1	.315/.391/.550
2018	HOU	MLB	23	468	60	20	1	15	65	53	111	3	0	.239/.323/.405
2019	*HOU*	*MLB*	*24*	*601*	*76*	*28*	*2*	*20*	*76*	*73*	*123*	*8*	*2*	*.264/.357/.441*

Breakout: 7%   Improve: 62%   Collapse: 5%   Attrition: 3%   MLB: 100%
Comparables: Hanley Ramirez, Corey Seager, David Wright

It's a testament to Houston's depth that they made it as far as they did in 2018 given all the key players that spent time on the disabled list. Along with such notable names as Altuve and Springer, Correa had his 2018 season diminished by injury, one that erased his July and ruined his batting line the rest of the season. Usually a mainstay in the heart of the Astros' lineup, Correa dealt with a lingering back issue that reduced him to ostensibly a below-average hitter in 2018. Backs are tricky things, but assuming he's healthy in 2019, there's no reason to expect he won't be back to his mashing ways again.

YEAR	TEAM	LVL	AGE	PA	DRC+	VORP	BABIP	BRR	FRAA	WARP
2016	HOU	MLB	21	660	124	53.7	.328	1.8	SS(153): -4.5	4.7
2017	HOU	MLB	22	481	140	47.4	.352	-3.0	SS(108): -1.4	4.1
2018	HOU	MLB	23	468	98	20.8	.282	0.8	SS(109): 7.2	2.8
2019	*HOU*	*MLB*	*24*	*601*	*122*	*38.9*	*.308*	*0.0*	*SS 2*	*4.0*

Carlos Correa, continued

Batted Ball Distribution

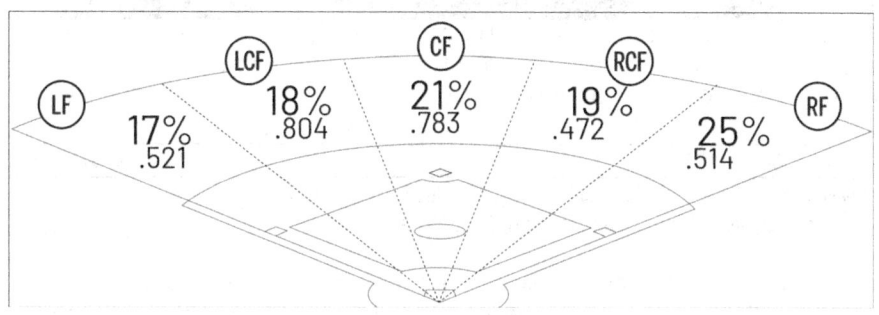

Strike Zone vs LHP   Strike Zone vs RHP

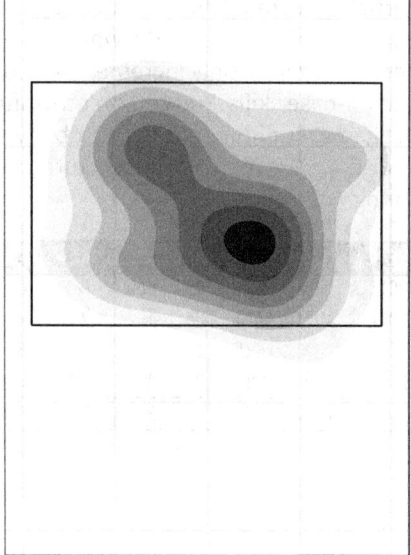

Aledmys Diaz INF

Born: 08/01/90 Age: 28 Bats: R Throws: R
Height: 6'1" Weight: 195 Origin: International Free Agent, 2014

YEAR	TEAM	LVL	AGE	PA	R	2B	3B	HR	RBI	BB	K	SB	CS	AVG/OBP/SLG
2016	SLN	MLB	25	460	71	28	3	17	65	41	60	4	4	.300/.369/.510
2017	MEM	AAA	26	187	19	9	1	4	26	10	30	3	3	.253/.305/.388
2017	SLN	MLB	26	301	31	17	0	7	20	13	42	4	1	.259/.290/.392
2018	TOR	MLB	27	452	55	26	0	18	55	23	62	3	4	.263/.303/.453
2019	HOU	MLB	28	351	40	17	1	10	39	25	53	4	3	.253/.311/.406

Breakout: 5% Improve: 49% Collapse: 6% Attrition: 7% MLB: 97%
Comparables: Alexei Ramirez, Didi Gregorius, Jordy Mercer

It can be difficult to divorce a seasoned player from his prospect profile. We want to believe the potential for greatness still lurks somewhere underneath a mediocre swing and lapsed velocity, and there's a certain defeat that comes with admitting the teenage superstar in the making is now little better than your garden-variety utility man. The Blue Jays scratched and scratched at that particular instant win ticket in 2018, but even given an everyday role (in the absence of Troy Tulowitzki, who lost the entire season to bone spurs in both heels), Diaz took only incremental steps forward to tweak his infield defense and on-base skills. You couldn't truthfully say that he excels at any one area of the game, but his positional flexibility and modest offensive totals were enough to intrigue the Astros, who will turn to him as their new Marwin Gonzalez come spring.

YEAR	TEAM	LVL	AGE	PA	DRC+	VORP	BABIP	BRR	FRAA	WARP
2016	SLN	MLB	25	460	125	48.7	.312	1.4	SS(106): -9.6, 2B(1): 0.0	2.6
2017	MEM	AAA	26	187	76	4.6	.281	-1.2	SS(28): 2.3, 3B(9): -0.6	0.2
2017	SLN	MLB	26	301	80	2.3	.282	-1.3	SS(68): -10.6, 3B(4): -0.2	-0.6
2018	TOR	MLB	27	452	108	19.2	.269	-1.8	SS(95): -5.8, 3B(38): -0.5	1.5
2019	HOU	MLB	28	351	100	12.0	.275	-0.7	SS -3, 2B 1	0.8

Aledmys Diaz, continued

Batted Ball Distribution

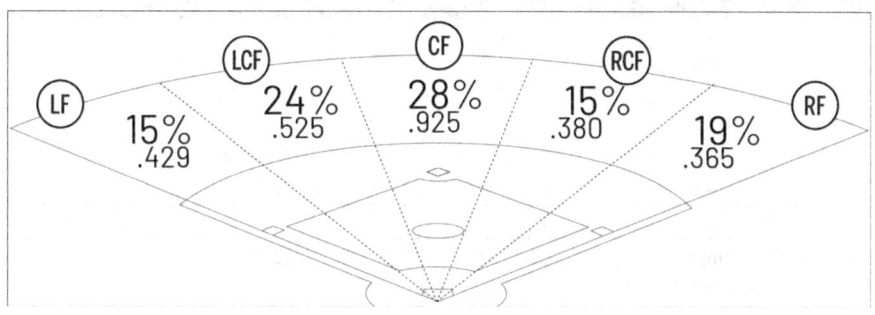

Strike Zone vs LHP

Strike Zone vs RHP

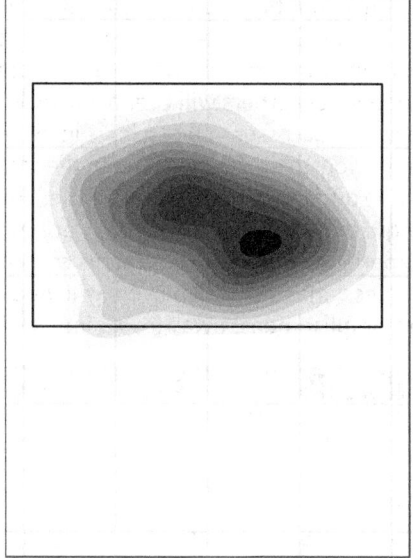

Houston Astros 2019

Derek Fisher OF

Born: 08/21/93 Age: 25 Bats: L Throws: R
Height: 6'3" Weight: 205 Origin: Round 1, 2014 Draft (#37 overall)

YEAR	TEAM	LVL	AGE	PA	R	2B	3B	HR	RBI	BB	K	SB	CS	AVG/OBP/SLG
2016	CCH	AA	22	448	54	13	4	16	59	74	128	23	7	.245/.373/.431
2016	FRE	AAA	22	118	17	8	0	5	17	9	26	5	0	.290/.347/.505
2017	FRE	AAA	23	384	63	26	1	21	66	35	74	16	10	.318/.384/.583
2017	HOU	MLB	23	166	21	4	1	5	17	17	54	3	3	.212/.307/.356
2018	HOU	MLB	24	86	13	2	2	4	11	5	42	2	0	.165/.209/.392
2018	FRE	AAA	24	281	44	12	1	10	34	39	85	11	1	.251/.363/.435
2019	HOU	MLB	25	120	16	5	0	5	14	11	35	3	1	.234/.308/.421

Breakout: 18% Improve: 44% Collapse: 13% Attrition: 36% MLB: 80%
Comparables: Bradley Zimmer, Joe Benson, Trayvon Robinson

Success in baseball can be measured in a thousand different ways. Getting drafted is a success. Being a first-round pick is an even bigger success. Showing up on a top prospect list is a success. Making the majors is a huge success. Getting your first major league hit, your first run, your first RBI, your first homer, all great successes. Making a playoff roster is a success. Scoring the game-winning run in one of the most memorable World Series games of all time is a success few others will ever achieve. Winning a World Series ring is one of the biggest successes you can have in all of sports. Derek Fisher's been an up-and-down fourth outfielder so far in the majors—an athletic guy who can play all three outfield spots and run a little, but hasn't hit much. He may well never be more than that. Yet he's already done all of the things listed above. He's experienced more success in his career to date than all but a small fraction of professional baseball players will. And you can't take any of those accomplishments away from him.

YEAR	TEAM	LVL	AGE	PA	DRC+	VORP	BABIP	BRR	FRAA	WARP
2016	CCH	AA	22	448	136	30.0	.329	-0.5	CF(70): -7.7, RF(19): -1.2	1.0
2016	FRE	AAA	22	118	114	8.2	.338	-0.6	RF(13): -1.6, CF(13): -0.9	0.0
2017	FRE	AAA	23	384	148	32.8	.352	-0.8	CF(53): -5.3, LF(17): 2.3	2.4
2017	HOU	MLB	23	166	70	-1.4	.299	-0.5	LF(38): 1.2, RF(12): 0.0	-0.1
2018	HOU	MLB	24	86	48	1.6	.257	1.6	LF(26): -1.3, CF(9): -0.4	-0.3
2018	FRE	AAA	24	281	114	16.5	.347	2.2	CF(33): -2.7, LF(19): -0.7	0.7
2019	HOU	MLB	25	120	94	2.7	.296	0.2	RF 0, LF 0	0.2

Derek Fisher, continued

Batted Ball Distribution

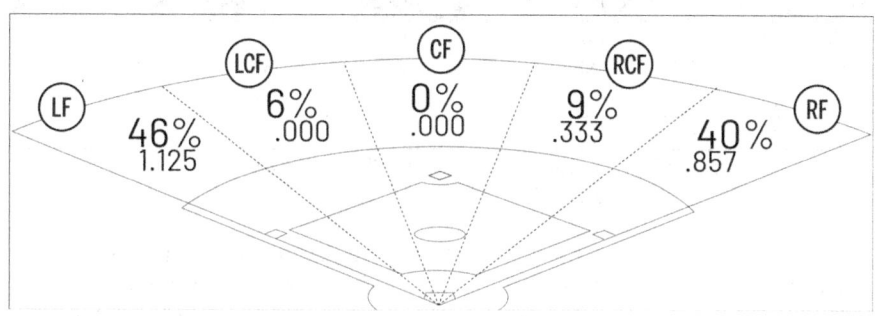

Strike Zone vs LHP **Strike Zone vs RHP**

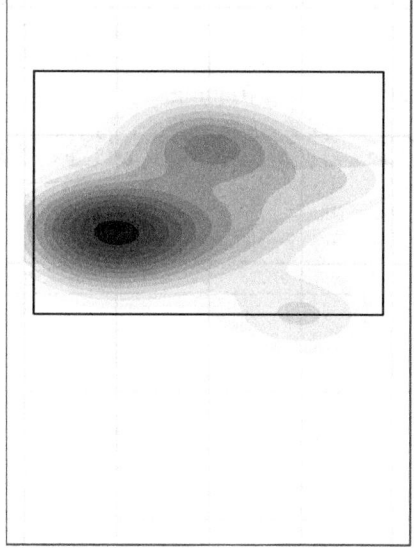

Yulieski Gurriel 1B

Born: 06/09/84 Age: 35 Bats: R Throws: R
Height: 6'0" Weight: 190 Origin: International Free Agent, 2016

YEAR	TEAM	LVL	AGE	PA	R	2B	3B	HR	RBI	BB	K	SB	CS	AVG/OBP/SLG
2016	HOU	MLB	32	137	13	7	0	3	15	5	12	1	1	.262/.292/.385
2017	HOU	MLB	33	564	69	43	1	18	75	22	62	3	2	.299/.332/.486
2018	HOU	MLB	34	573	70	33	1	13	85	23	63	5	1	.291/.323/.428
2019	HOU	MLB	35	565	58	31	2	13	63	32	74	4	2	.270/.318/.412

Breakout: 2%   Improve: 19%   Collapse: 25%   Attrition: 25%   MLB: 85%
Comparables: Bill Buckner, Ross Gload, Mike Sweeney

In his second full season since defecting from Cuba, Gurriel wasn't able to repeat his 2017 output. Though the ball was softer for everyone, it wasn't helped by the fact that he hit into 22 double plays in 2018, as he chased (and succeeded in putting the bat on) more bad pitches in 2018. Somewhat paradoxically, most of those occurred in the first half of the season, the half in which he actually hit much better. Baseball, like life, is devoid of any understanding and this only proves it further. Gurriel also stunk up the joint in the 2018 postseason, and was arguably the worst hitter in the regular lineup (save for the catching position), so don't be surprised if he feels the pressure as early as Spring Training.

YEAR	TEAM	LVL	AGE	PA	DRC+	VORP	BABIP	BRR	FRAA	WARP
2016	HOU	MLB	32	137	98	-3.0	.267	-1.2	3B(21): -0.8, 1B(5): 0.1	0.1
2017	HOU	MLB	33	564	109	18.0	.308	-1.7	1B(131): 8.4, 3B(7): -0.3	2.1
2018	HOU	MLB	34	573	109	20.7	.306	1.1	1B(109): 1.5, 3B(21): 1.2	2.0
2019	HOU	MLB	35	565	100	10.8	.292	-0.7	1B 4, RF 0	1.5

Yulieski Gurriel, continued

Batted Ball Distribution

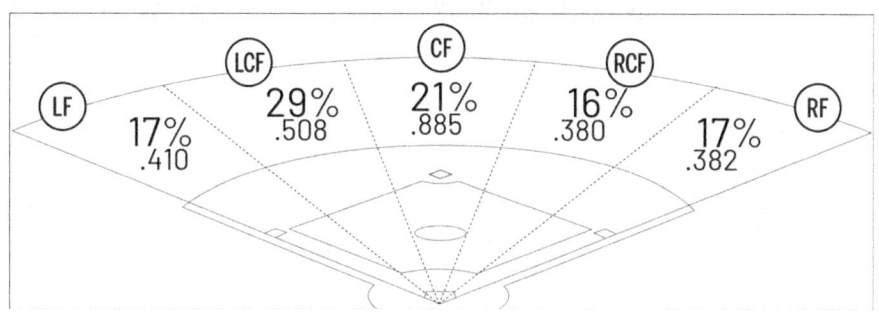

Strike Zone vs LHP   Strike Zone vs RHP

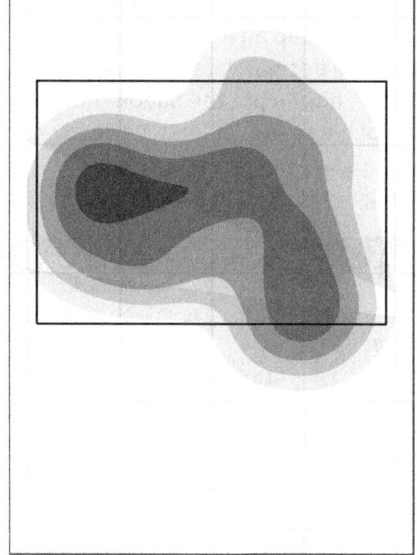

Astros Player Analysis - 33

Tony Kemp LF

Born: 10/31/91   Age: 27   Bats: L   Throws: R
Height: 5'6"   Weight: 165   Origin: Round 5, 2013 Draft (#137 overall)

YEAR	TEAM	LVL	AGE	PA	R	2B	3B	HR	RBI	BB	K	SB	CS	AVG/OBP/SLG
2016	FRE	AAA	24	301	36	9	4	2	24	34	34	10	8	.306/.389/.396
2016	HOU	MLB	24	136	15	4	3	1	7	14	27	2	1	.217/.296/.325
2017	FRE	AAA	25	554	95	23	9	10	62	35	43	24	7	.329/.375/.470
2017	HOU	MLB	25	39	6	1	0	0	4	1	5	1	0	.216/.256/.243
2018	FRE	AAA	26	183	33	6	5	0	19	19	15	13	2	.335/.407/.435
2018	HOU	MLB	26	295	37	15	0	6	30	32	44	9	3	.263/.351/.392
2019	HOU	MLB	27	211	25	8	2	5	21	17	33	6	2	.265/.330/.407

Breakout: 5%   Improve: 35%   Collapse: 2%   Attrition: 25%   MLB: 72%
Comparables: Jeremy Reed, J.B. Shuck, Guillermo Heredia

Kemp will always draw comparisons to Jose Altuve due to the facts that he is a smaller gentleman and he plays for the Houston Astros. Chances are he won't be able to change the former, and given his very respectable stint on the 2018 squad, the Astros might want to keep him around for a while. Kemp got the call in May to help an injury-plagued outfield and played serviceable defense while showing decent plate discipline and even knocked a handful of dingers. Like Altuve, he can put the bat on the ball quite well, and though he's not the same tier of hitter, he's at least a selective one. He can hold down the bottom end of a lineup, and will probably see plenty of left field unless Derek Fisher makes the leap, or one of Houston's stud prospects starts making a lot of noise.

YEAR	TEAM	LVL	AGE	PA	DRC+	VORP	BABIP	BRR	FRAA	WARP
2016	FRE	AAA	24	301	106	12.7	.344	0.2	2B(39): -0.1, LF(19): 2.3	0.7
2016	HOU	MLB	24	136	82	-2.5	.269	-0.4	LF(37): -2.5, 2B(5): 0.0	-0.3
2017	FRE	AAA	25	554	113	39.1	.344	0.4	2B(97): -10.2, LF(10): -1.4	0.7
2017	HOU	MLB	25	39	91	-1.7	.250	0.9	LF(10): -0.4, CF(4): -0.2	0.1
2018	FRE	AAA	26	183	111	14.6	.367	3.5	2B(25): -0.5, CF(14): -1.4	0.7
2018	HOU	MLB	26	295	105	9.6	.296	-0.5	LF(61): -2.8, CF(32): 0.3	0.7
2019	HOU	MLB	27	211	97	6.6	.288	0.6	LF -1, CF -2	0.4

Tony Kemp, continued

Batted Ball Distribution

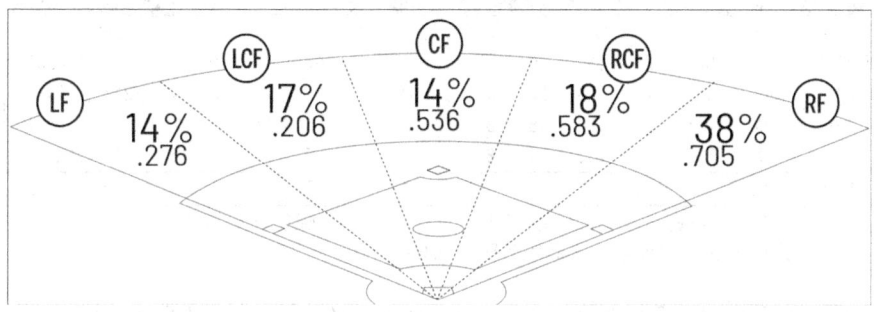

Strike Zone vs LHP   Strike Zone vs RHP

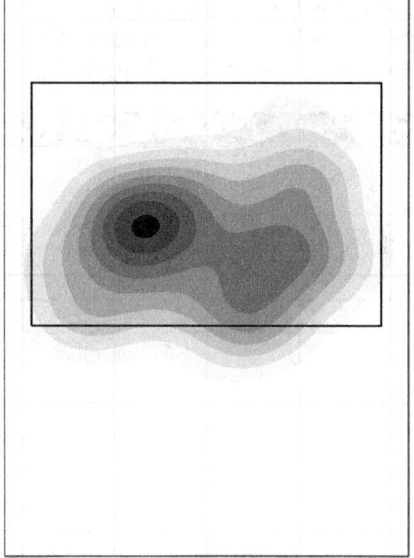

Jake Marisnick CF

Born: 03/30/91 Age: 28 Bats: R Throws: R
Height: 6'4" Weight: 220 Origin: Round 3, 2009 Draft (#104 overall)

YEAR	TEAM	LVL	AGE	PA	R	2B	3B	HR	RBI	BB	K	SB	CS	AVG/OBP/SLG
2016	FRE	AAA	25	28	3	2	0	0	1	1	10	1	1	.185/.214/.259
2016	HOU	MLB	25	311	40	18	1	5	21	16	83	10	5	.209/.257/.331
2017	HOU	MLB	26	259	50	10	0	16	35	20	90	9	4	.243/.319/.496
2018	FRE	AAA	27	82	18	8	2	4	13	6	17	3	1	.342/.402/.671
2018	HOU	MLB	27	235	34	8	1	10	28	15	84	6	2	.211/.275/.399
2019	HOU	MLB	28	122	16	5	0	4	13	9	36	5	2	.220/.289/.376

Breakout: 4% Improve: 39% Collapse: 13% Attrition: 13% MLB: 89%
Comparables: Peter Bourjos, Mikie Mahtook, Franklin Gutierrez

How can such a good-looking man have such ugly at-bats? Marisnick, who is very handsome, made a complete 180 on his promising 2017 campaign and fell flat on his very attractive face in 2018. Long regarded as an angelic defensive replacement, Marisnick looked to have gotten over a hump in 2017 when he complimented his poor plate discipline with some real power numbers. But much like Cinderella's carriage, this beautiful thing turned back into a pumpkin. He's very pleasing to look at, is what we're saying.

YEAR	TEAM	LVL	AGE	PA	DRC+	VORP	BABIP	BRR	FRAA	WARP
2016	FRE	AAA	25	28	26	-2.0	.294	-0.1	CF(6): 0.4, RF(2): 0.1	-0.1
2016	HOU	MLB	25	311	63	-6.2	.275	-1.1	CF(74): 8.8, LF(26): 1.4	0.5
2017	HOU	MLB	26	259	95	13.8	.320	1.4	CF(93): -5.2, LF(6): 0.3	0.4
2018	FRE	AAA	27	82	169	10.2	.396	-0.5	CF(12): -2.3, RF(6): 0.9	0.5
2018	HOU	MLB	27	235	80	6.0	.292	2.3	CF(96): -5.7, RF(1): 0.0	-0.1
2019	HOU	MLB	28	122	89	3.5	.289	0.3	CF -1	0.2

Jake Marisnick, continued

Batted Ball Distribution

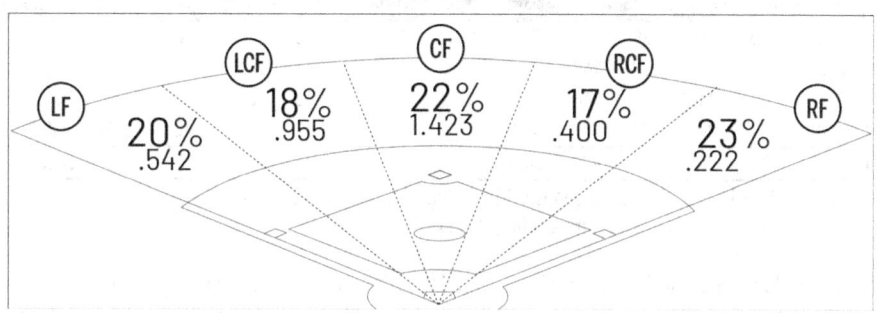

Strike Zone vs LHP

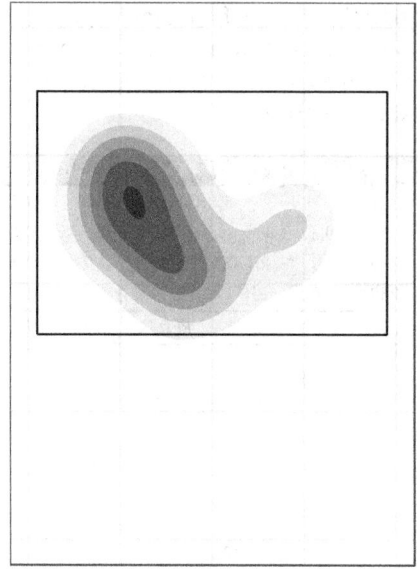

Strike Zone vs RHP

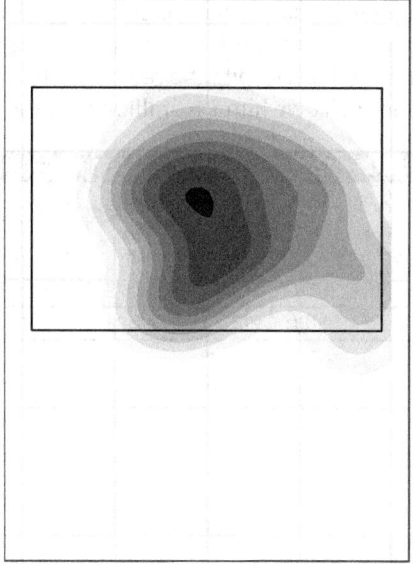

Josh Reddick RF

Born: 02/19/87 Age: 32 Bats: L Throws: R
Height: 6'2" Weight: 195 Origin: Round 17, 2006 Draft (#523 overall)

YEAR	TEAM	LVL	AGE	PA	R	2B	3B	HR	RBI	BB	K	SB	CS	AVG/OBP/SLG
2016	OAK	MLB	29	272	33	11	1	8	28	28	34	5	0	.296/.368/.449
2016	LAN	MLB	29	167	20	6	0	2	9	11	22	3	3	.258/.307/.335
2017	HOU	MLB	30	540	77	34	4	13	82	43	72	7	3	.314/.363/.484
2018	HOU	MLB	31	487	63	13	2	17	47	49	77	7	2	.242/.318/.400
2019	HOU	MLB	32	441	50	22	2	11	51	39	73	6	2	.272/.338/.421

Breakout: 1% Improve: 33% Collapse: 12% Attrition: 8% MLB: 98%
Comparables: David DeJesus, Tommy Griffith, Dixie Walker

Reddick's OPS sank by 129 points in 2018. Oddly enough, nothing about his plate discipline changed all that much, nor did his contact or walk rate. Most of the difference can be chalked up to a seemingly uncharacteristic .258 BABIP, despite nearly identical batted ball rates. In previous years, we'd see this as a harbinger for pending regression. However, there's another element now: Reddick's batted ball velocity, usually around the median for major leaguers, dropped to a tenth-percentile 85.2 mph, and he's barreling it up less often then he used to. Despite the red flags, Houston is forced to hope for a rebound, as they still owe him $26 million over the next two seasons.

YEAR	TEAM	LVL	AGE	PA	DRC+	VORP	BABIP	BRR	FRAA	WARP
2016	OAK	MLB	29	272	110	18.0	.317	2.1	RF(68): 3.0	1.4
2016	LAN	MLB	29	167	112	-0.7	.290	-0.3	RF(42): 0.8	0.6
2017	HOU	MLB	30	540	119	33.3	.339	2.5	RF(102): -1.6, LF(48): -1.2	2.4
2018	HOU	MLB	31	487	106	10.7	.258	-1.0	RF(111): -2.0, LF(43): 0.4	1.2
2019	HOU	MLB	32	441	108	18.3	.312	0.0	RF 0	1.6

Josh Reddick, continued

Batted Ball Distribution

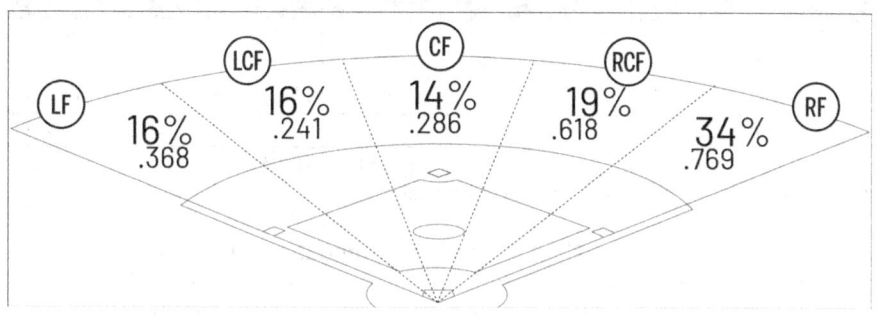

Strike Zone vs LHP **Strike Zone vs RHP**

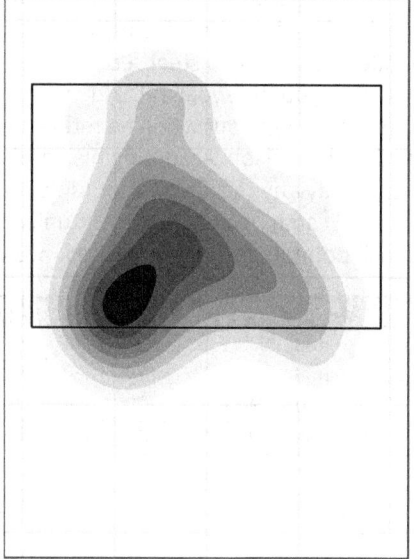

George Springer RF

Born: 09/19/89 Age: 29 Bats: R Throws: R
Height: 6'3" Weight: 215 Origin: Round 1, 2011 Draft (#11 overall)

YEAR	TEAM	LVL	AGE	PA	R	2B	3B	HR	RBI	BB	K	SB	CS	AVG/OBP/SLG
2016	HOU	MLB	26	744	116	29	5	29	82	88	178	9	10	.261/.359/.457
2017	HOU	MLB	27	629	112	29	0	34	85	64	111	5	7	.283/.367/.522
2018	HOU	MLB	28	620	102	26	0	22	71	64	122	6	4	.265/.346/.434
2019	HOU	MLB	29	655	94	27	2	24	76	75	132	8	6	.257/.353/.439

Breakout: 3% Improve: 46% Collapse: 13% Attrition: 5% MLB: 96%
Comparables: Carlos Beltran, Chet Lemon, Grady Sizemore

There's a longstanding and highly-unsubstantiated theory that the one injury that can sap a batter's power more than any other is a hand injury. This seems a little weird given all the moving muscles, joints, bones and chitin that go into a baseball swing. But the hands are the body's connector to the bat and our world is built upon a bedrock of unanswerable questions, so here we are.

Regardless of the scientific reasoning behind said theory, Springer would a be a prime candidate in proving its validity. An early-August thumb sprain suffered while attempting to steal second stalled what was promising to be another highly productive year. All told, he missed only as many games as he did in his 2017 campaign, but when he returned he wasn't *George Springer* until the very end of the season. Assuming his hands are all healed up by next season, there isn't really any reason he shouldn't have another productive year in 2019. His age will catch up with him eventually—but it will for all of us and there's not much point in giving in to those kinds of thoughts.

YEAR	TEAM	LVL	AGE	PA	DRC+	VORP	BABIP	BRR	FRAA	WARP
2016	HOU	MLB	26	744	124	29.4	.317	1.2	RF(147): 20.1, CF(1): 0.0	5.9
2017	HOU	MLB	27	629	130	40.8	.297	0.5	CF(84): 2.6, RF(78): 0.6	4.5
2018	HOU	MLB	28	620	114	30.6	.303	1.5	CF(80): -2.8, RF(77): 2.6	2.9
2019	HOU	MLB	29	655	120	40.9	.293	-1.6	CF -5, RF 2	3.4

George Springer, continued

Batted Ball Distribution

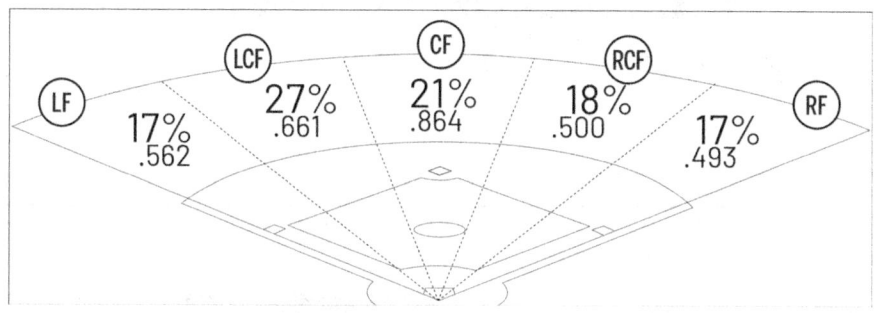

Strike Zone vs LHP

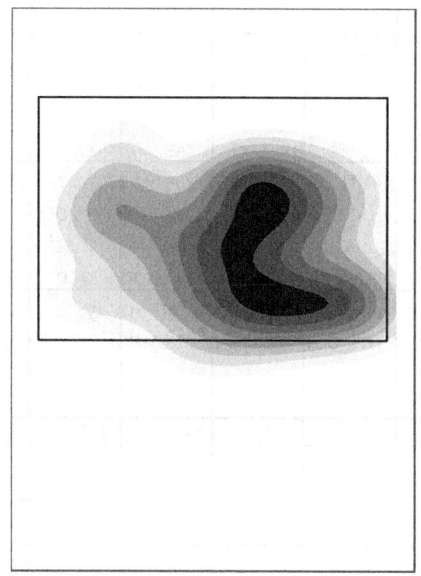

Strike Zone vs RHP

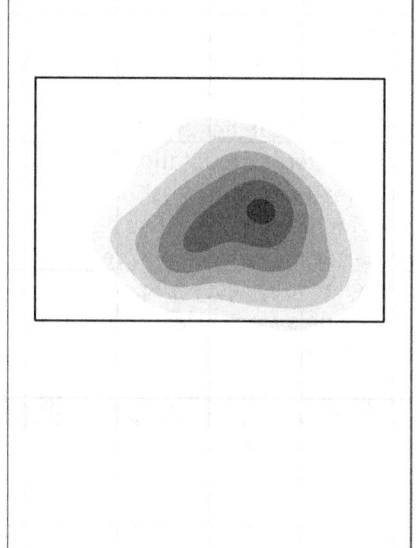

Max Stassi C

Born: 03/15/91   Age: 28   Bats: R   Throws: R
Height: 5'10"   Weight: 200   Origin: Round 4, 2009 Draft (#123 overall)

YEAR	TEAM	LVL	AGE	PA	R	2B	3B	HR	RBI	BB	K	SB	CS	AVG/OBP/SLG
2016	FRE	AAA	25	266	21	12	1	7	32	20	65	1	0	.230/.294/.374
2016	HOU	MLB	25	13	1	0	0	0	0	0	5	0	0	.077/.077/.077
2017	FRE	AAA	26	287	54	14	0	12	33	38	67	1	1	.266/.383/.473
2017	HOU	MLB	26	31	5	1	0	2	4	6	4	0	0	.167/.323/.458
2018	HOU	MLB	27	250	28	13	0	8	27	23	74	0	0	.226/.316/.394
2019	HOU	MLB	28	258	28	10	1	8	29	23	69	0	0	.218/.300/.376

Breakout: 6%   Improve: 32%   Collapse: 5%   Attrition: 32%   MLB: 53%
Comparables: Chris Gimenez, John Baker, Jose Lobaton

YEAR	TEAM	P. COUNT	FRM RUNS	BLK RUNS	THRW RUNS	TOT RUNS
2016	HOU	491	-0.3	0.1	0.0	0.2
2017	FRE	9878	11.4	0.0	-0.8	10.1
2017	HOU	1029	0.2	0.4	0.0	0.5
2018	HOU	9540	13.9	0.1	-0.1	14.0
2019	HOU	9995	8.8	-0.1	-0.4	8.3

What do we owe to a backup catcher? After five straight years spent mostly sitting around Triple-A as Houston's third catcher/Mindy St. Claire—getting MLB time every year but maxing out at 31 plate appearances in 2017—Stassi *finally* broke out of The Medium Place and established himself as a bona fide MLB backup catcher in 2018. He posted strong defensive numbers to go along with the sterling reputation he'd developed in the high minors, and surpassed the "greater than useless" offensive threshold for a reserve catcher. The good news for Stassi as he enters his late twenties is that once you're established as a viable backup catcher, you've got a shot to hang around in The Good Place long enough to fully vest your pension. The bad news is that Janet can always conjure up a Martin Maldonado in a trade if you don't keep accumulating those good person points, or if your framing slips a little.

YEAR	TEAM	LVL	AGE	PA	DRC+	VORP	BABIP	BRR	FRAA	WARP
2016	FRE	AAA	25	266	71	5.1	.287	1.1	C(66): 8.5	1.0
2016	HOU	MLB	25	13	66	-2.3	.125	-0.1	C(8): -0.3	0.0
2017	FRE	AAA	26	287	127	26.3	.321	-0.2	C(65): 10.8	2.9
2017	HOU	MLB	26	31	106	0.9	.105	0.0	C(11): 0.5, 1B(1): 0.0	0.2
2018	HOU	MLB	27	250	86	9.8	.302	-0.1	C(82): 14.5	2.3
2019	HOU	MLB	28	258	84	7.2	.268	-0.5	C 7	1.3

Max Stassi, continued

Batted Ball Distribution

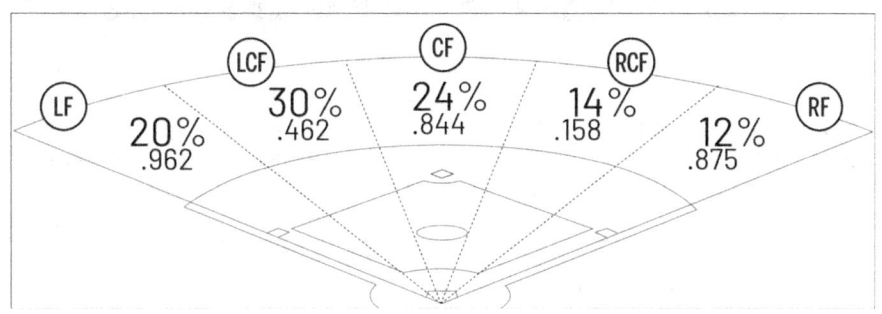

Strike Zone vs LHP   Strike Zone vs RHP

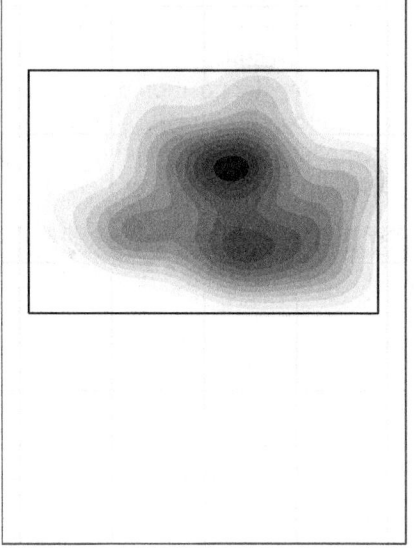

Kyle Tucker OF

Born: 01/17/97 Age: 22 Bats: L Throws: R
Height: 6'4" Weight: 190 Origin: Round 1, 2015 Draft (#5 overall)

YEAR	TEAM	LVL	AGE	PA	R	2B	3B	HR	RBI	BB	K	SB	CS	AVG/OBP/SLG
2016	QUD	A	19	428	43	19	5	6	56	40	75	31	9	.276/.348/.402
2016	LNC	A+	19	69	13	6	2	3	13	10	6	1	3	.339/.435/.661
2017	BCA	A+	20	206	31	12	4	9	43	24	45	13	5	.288/.379/.554
2017	CCH	AA	20	318	39	21	1	16	47	22	64	8	4	.265/.325/.512
2018	FRE	AAA	21	465	86	27	3	24	93	48	84	20	4	.332/.400/.590
2018	HOU	MLB	21	72	10	2	1	0	4	6	13	1	1	.141/.236/.203
2019	HOU	MLB	22	291	41	16	1	13	39	23	66	8	3	.270/.331/.487

Breakout: 18% Improve: 55% Collapse: 1% Attrition: 15% MLB: 62%
Comparables: Oswaldo Arcia, Tyler Austin, Joc Pederson

Way back in 2015, the Astros signed Tucker to a below-slot deal to save money to sign fellow prep outfielder Daz Cameron with a supplemental pick. That decision has already paid off twice over, with Cameron as a key component in the Justin Verlander trade that led to a World Series win, and Tucker emerging into one of the top prospects in all the land. He didn't do a whole lot of damage in three short stints in the majors, but he hit the snot out of the ball as one of the youngest regular position players in Triple-A. The perceived bar for success for an elite prospect is higher than it's ever been right now because of all of the incredible hitting performances put up by top prospects graduating to the majors. This one just might clear it.

YEAR	TEAM	LVL	AGE	PA	DRC+	VORP	BABIP	BRR	FRAA	WARP
2016	QUD	A	19	428	127	20.9	.322	1.3	CF(61): -5.2, LF(17): -0.3	1.3
2016	LNC	A+	19	69	178	8.0	.340	0.2	RF(6): -0.1, LF(4): 0.2	0.5
2017	BCA	A+	20	206	144	21.3	.336	-3.1	RF(19): -1.8, CF(17): 1.2	0.6
2017	CCH	AA	20	318	132	19.6	.286	1.2	CF(37): -5.3, RF(18): -1.4	0.6
2018	FRE	AAA	21	465	160	52.8	.364	1.7	RF(54): 0.3, LF(32): -0.4	3.6
2018	HOU	MLB	21	72	73	-5.7	.176	-0.4	LF(20): -2.1, RF(3): 0.2	-0.3
2019	HOU	MLB	22	291	122	17.1	.316	0.5	LF -4, RF 0	1.3

Kyle Tucker, continued

Batted Ball Distribution

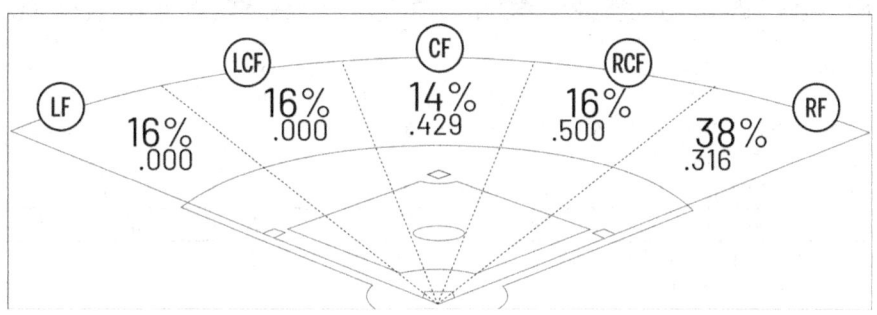

Strike Zone vs LHP   **Strike Zone vs RHP**

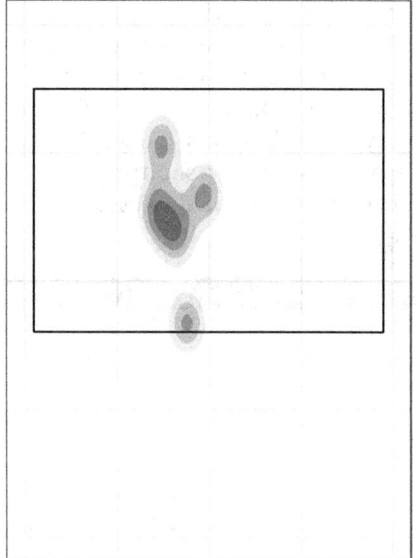

Tyler White 1B

Born: 10/29/90   Age: 28   Bats: R   Throws: R
Height: 5'11"   Weight: 225   Origin: Round 33, 2013 Draft (#977 overall)

YEAR	TEAM	LVL	AGE	PA	R	2B	3B	HR	RBI	BB	K	SB	CS	AVG/OBP/SLG
2016	FRE	AAA	25	190	28	4	1	13	29	16	30	1	1	.241/.305/.500
2016	HOU	MLB	25	276	24	16	0	8	28	23	65	1	0	.217/.286/.378
2017	FRE	AAA	26	497	84	22	1	25	89	47	101	7	3	.300/.371/.528
2017	HOU	MLB	26	67	7	6	0	3	10	4	16	0	1	.279/.328/.525
2018	FRE	AAA	27	313	55	18	0	14	53	46	39	1	1	.333/.444/.569
2018	HOU	MLB	27	237	27	12	3	12	42	24	49	0	1	.276/.354/.533
2019	HOU	MLB	28	238	29	10	1	10	32	22	51	1	1	.255/.331/.453

Breakout: 5%   Improve: 37%   Collapse: 16%   Attrition: 28%   MLB: 78%
Comparables: Justin Bour, Chris Parmelee, Tyler Moore

Back in the simpler days of 2016, White flamed out in an early-season shot at the MLB starting first base job. We said last year that the long-time minors masher deserved another shot to graduate to The Show, and he parlayed another hot first half in Triple-A into regular playing time after the Astros were struck by the injury bug. This time, he grabbed the brass ring and thrived. Even when all the regulars came back for the playoffs, he still had a role as a platoon DH and pinch-hitter. This is a fairly fungible profile these days, but he's still a few years away from arbitration. It doesn't hurt that he'll pitch in blowouts and stand at second base or even shortstop when you ask him, either. He's already made it further than you could've ever imagined for a 33rd-round senior sign from Western Carolina.

YEAR	TEAM	LVL	AGE	PA	DRC+	VORP	BABIP	BRR	FRAA	WARP
2016	FRE	AAA	25	190	121	5.8	.221	-1.2	1B(24): 0.9, SS(3): 0.3	0.3
2016	HOU	MLB	25	276	88	-3.7	.258	-0.1	1B(58): -2.5, 3B(3): 0.0	-0.3
2017	FRE	AAA	26	497	133	40.6	.334	0.5	3B(50): 8.3, 2B(21): -0.2	3.8
2017	HOU	MLB	26	67	98	4.5	.326	0.4	1B(19): -1.5, 2B(4): 0.1	0.0
2018	FRE	AAA	27	313	179	30.5	.345	-2.7	2B(26): 0.0, 3B(23): 1.5	3.1
2018	HOU	MLB	27	237	126	16.9	.307	-2.2	1B(42): 0.6	0.9
2019	HOU	MLB	28	238	112	7.5	.282	-0.4	1B -1	0.7

Tyler White, continued

Batted Ball Distribution

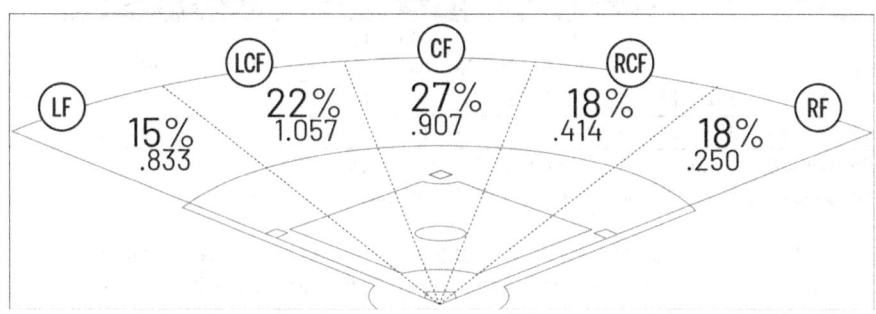

Strike Zone vs LHP   **Strike Zone vs RHP**

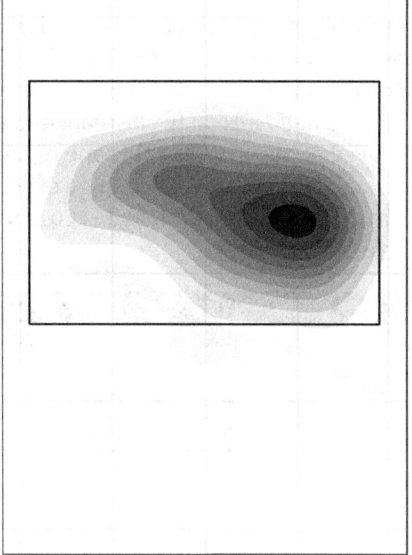

Gerrit Cole RHP

Born: 09/08/90   Age: 28   Bats: R   Throws: R
Height: 6'4"   Weight: 225   Origin: Round 1, 2011 Draft (#1 overall)

YEAR	TEAM	LVL	AGE	W	L	SV	G	GS	IP	H	HR	BB/9	K/9	K	GB%	BABIP
2016	PIT	MLB	25	7	10	0	21	21	116	131	7	2.8	7.6	98	48%	.345
2017	PIT	MLB	26	12	12	0	33	33	203	199	31	2.4	8.7	196	47%	.298
2018	HOU	MLB	27	15	5	0	32	32	200¹	143	19	2.9	12.4	276	38%	.286
2019	HOU	MLB	28	14	7	0	29	29	182²	153	20	2.8	10.7	216	42%	.296

Breakout: 20%   Improve: 59%   Collapse: 21%   Attrition: 4%   MLB: 95%
Comparables: Josh Beckett, Madison Bumgarner, Yovani Gallardo

The Astros gave up a hefty package—at least in terms of number of players and name recognition of said players—to acquire Cole prior to the 2018 season. Judging trades this early and judging trades in general is kind of a silly exercise, but it is safe to say that Houston was content with the pitcher they received in the form of 2018 Gerrit Cole.

Cole produced the highest strikeout rate of his major-league career—by a pretty big margin, actually. His underlying numbers didn't change all that much save for one thing: a more-utilized and faster fastball. An age-27 Gerrit Cole, who was not moved to the bullpen or coming off any kind of known injury, actually gained a half MPH on his fastball. And it doesn't take a highly respected and beloved publication like this one to tell you, the reader, that this is just kind of... strange. Perhaps it was a change of scenery, perhaps Cole has starting meddling in the dark arts. Regardless, his 2018 season was his best by pretty much every measure.

YEAR	TEAM	LVL	AGE	WHIP	ERA	DRA	WARP	MPH	FB%	WHF	CSP
2016	PIT	MLB	25	1.44	3.88	4.42	1.2	98.3	66.8	9.1	48.6
2017	PIT	MLB	26	1.25	4.26	3.84	3.9	98.0	60	10.1	49.5
2018	HOU	MLB	27	1.03	2.88	2.55	6.4	98.7	56.3	15.3	49.8
2019	HOU	MLB	28	1.16	3.30	3.64	3.8	97.8	59.8	12.4	49.7

Gerrit Cole, continued

Pitch Shape vs LHH

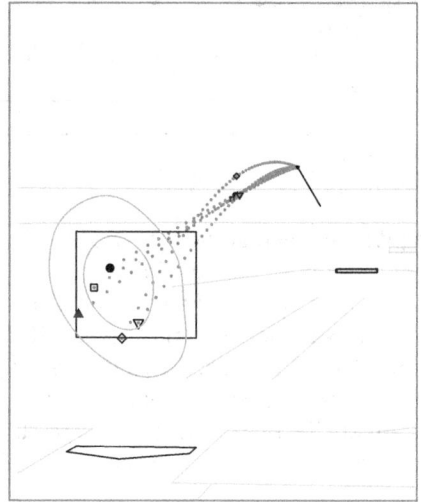

Pitch Shape vs RHH

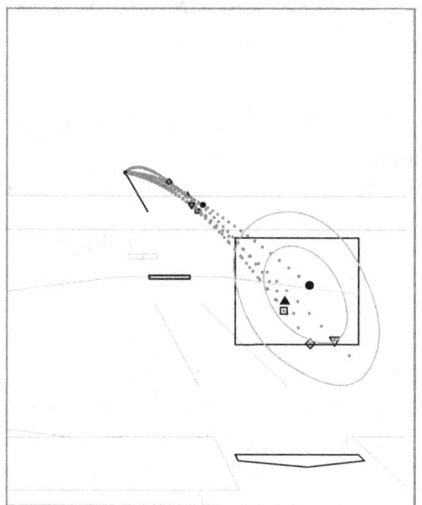

Type	Frequency	Velocity	H Movement	V Movement
● Fastball	53.4%	97 [114]	-9.6 [86]	-11.2 [114]
☐ Sinker	3.0%	96.6 [120]	-13.8 [90]	-15.3 [116]
+ Cutter				
▲ Changeup	4.5%	88.2 [112]	-12.3 [94]	-21.8 [116]
✕ Splitter				
▽ Slider	19.9%	89.1 [121]	5 [100]	-27.3 [117]
◇ Curveball	19.3%	82.9 [116]	11.4 [115]	-45.9 [105]
⊕ Slow Curveball				
✱ Knuckleball				
▼ Screwball				

Chris Devenski   RHP

Born: 11/13/90   Age: 28   Bats: R   Throws: R
Height: 6'3"   Weight: 210   Origin: Round 25, 2011 Draft (#771 overall)

YEAR	TEAM	LVL	AGE	W	L	SV	G	GS	IP	H	HR	BB/9	K/9	K	GB%	BABIP
2016	HOU	MLB	25	4	4	1	48	5	108^1	79	4	1.7	8.6	104	34%	.271
2017	HOU	MLB	26	8	5	4	62	0	80^2	50	11	2.9	11.2	100	41%	.220
2018	HOU	MLB	27	2	3	2	50	1	47^1	42	9	2.5	9.7	51	37%	.275
2019	HOU	MLB	28	3	2	0	52	0	54	44	6	3.0	9.9	60	38%	.279

Breakout: 20%   Improve: 42%   Collapse: 28%   Attrition: 23%   MLB: 92%
Comparables: Andrew Bailey, Hunter Strickland, Zack Godley

Devenski's two-year run of being a dominant high-leverage reliever was foiled by a hamstring injury that put him on the shelf for over a month. When he returned late in the season, he found that his role had been filled by others, a fact that found him sitting out the entire 2018 postseason. Entering his age-28 season, he's still a young man, and has shown truly dominant stuff over the past couple of years. That stuff is unchanged, but there are a few worrying trends—a higher contact rate in the zone and an accompanying rise in homers—that he'll need to iron out to reclaim his status as the Right-Handed Andrew Miller.

YEAR	TEAM	LVL	AGE	WHIP	ERA	DRA	WARP	MPH	FB%	WHF	CSP
2016	HOU	MLB	25	0.91	2.16	2.78	2.8	95.6	45.8	14.5	47.2
2017	HOU	MLB	26	0.94	2.68	3.09	1.9	95.5	39.7	17.7	45.9
2018	HOU	MLB	27	1.16	4.18	3.61	0.7	95.9	41.6	15.2	46.7
2019	HOU	MLB	28	1.12	3.39	3.86	0.8	95.1	42.6	16	46.9

Chris Devenski, continued

Pitch Shape vs LHH

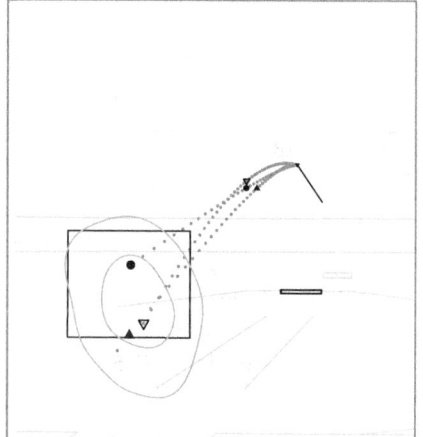

Pitch Shape vs RHH

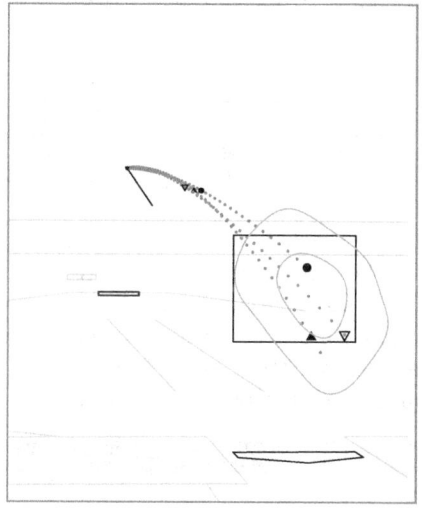

Type	Frequency	Velocity	H Movement	V Movement
● Fastball	41.5%	94.5 [106]	-10.6 [82]	-14.6 [104]
☐ Sinker				
+ Cutter				
▲ Changeup	39.1%	83.3 [92]	-12.9 [91]	-33.2 [83]
✕ Splitter				
▽ Slider	19.4%	82.3 [90]	6.9 [109]	-34.1 [97]
◇ Curveball				
⊕ Slow Curveball				
✳ Knuckleball				
▼ Screwball				

Astros Player Analysis - 51

Will Harris RHP

Born: 08/28/84   Age: 34   Bats: R   Throws: R
Height: 6'4"   Weight: 250   Origin: Round 9, 2006 Draft (#258 overall)

YEAR	TEAM	LVL	AGE	W	L	SV	G	GS	IP	H	HR	BB/9	K/9	K	GB%	BABIP
2016	HOU	MLB	31	1	2	12	66	0	64	52	3	2.1	9.7	69	59%	.293
2017	HOU	MLB	32	3	2	2	46	0	45^1	37	7	1.4	10.3	52	49%	.270
2018	HOU	MLB	33	5	3	0	61	0	56^2	48	3	2.2	10.2	64	54%	.306
2019	HOU	MLB	34	3	2	0	52	0	54	46	6	2.9	9.6	58	51%	.282

Breakout: 12%   Improve: 29%   Collapse: 39%   Attrition: 8%   MLB: 87%
Comparables: Heath Bell, Francisco Cordero, Scott Downs

In 2018, Harris had a very similar season to his 2017 effort, which is to say it was very, very good. He stranded fewer batters, and his peripherals saw some light decay, but he made up for it by drastically reducing his home run rate. In the baseball roster equivalent of lighting cigars with hundred dollar bills, the reliever-rich Astros elected not to pick up Harris's very affordable $5.5 million option for 2019, but he remains under team control.

YEAR	TEAM	LVL	AGE	WHIP	ERA	DRA	WARP	MPH	FB%	WHF	CSP
2016	HOU	MLB	31	1.05	2.25	2.26	2.0	94.6	66.4	14.4	45
2017	HOU	MLB	32	0.97	2.98	2.45	1.4	93.2	68.7	13.9	46.9
2018	HOU	MLB	33	1.09	3.49	2.32	1.7	93.5	62.3	14.5	42.5
2019	HOU	MLB	34	1.14	3.30	3.78	0.9	92.6	64.3	14.1	43.9

Will Harris, continued

Pitch Shape vs LHH
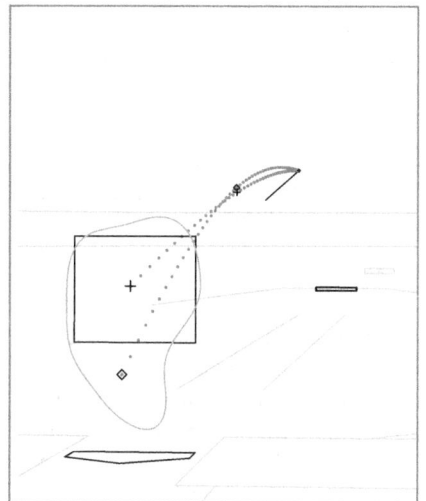

Pitch Shape vs RHH
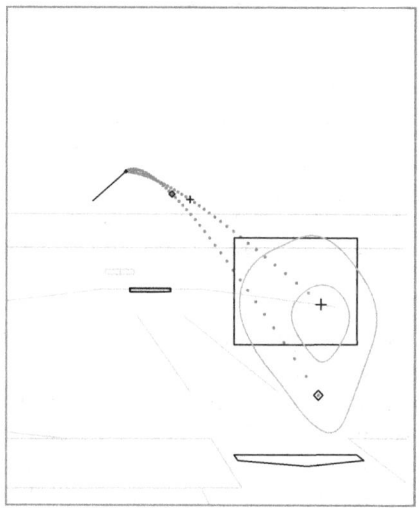

Type	Frequency	Velocity	H Movement	V Movement
● Fastball	0.3%	92.9 [101]	-8 [94]	-19.7 [88]
□ Sinker				
+ Cutter	62.0%	92.5 [122]	3.6 [110]	-19.4 [117]
▲ Changeup				
× Splitter				
▽ Slider				
◇ Curveball	37.7%	82.9 [116]	11.6 [116]	-48.1 [100]
⊕ Slow Curveball				
✶ Knuckleball				
▼ Screwball				

Josh James RHP

Born: 03/08/93   Age: 26   Bats: R   Throws: R
Height: 6'3"   Weight: 206   Origin: Round 34, 2014 Draft (#1006 overall)

YEAR	TEAM	LVL	AGE	W	L	SV	G	GS	IP	H	HR	BB/9	K/9	K	GB%	BABIP
2016	LNC	A+	23	9	5	1	23	19	110^1	120	11	3.3	9.9	121	48%	.350
2017	CCH	AA	24	4	8	3	21	11	76	79	1	3.8	8.5	72	53%	.338
2018	CCH	AA	25	0	0	1	6	4	21^2	17	1	4.2	15.8	38	58%	.364
2018	FRE	AAA	25	6	4	0	17	17	92^2	62	8	3.8	12.9	133	41%	.278
2018	HOU	MLB	25	2	0	0	6	3	23	15	3	2.7	11.3	29	42%	.240
2019	HOU	MLB	26	6	4	0	51	10	93	76	9	3.8	10.7	112	44%	.292

Breakout: 17%   Improve: 34%   Collapse: 17%   Attrition: 33%   MLB: 62%
Comparables: Tom Mastny, Adam Conley, D.J. Snelten

Most of the world got introduced to James during the 2018 ALCS, and, well, it could have gone better for him. However, the young flamethrower had a good run during his late-season call up, save for a slight home run problem. James was almost exclusively a starter in the minors, but Houston may look to utilize his high-90s fastball and mid-80s changeup in the bullpen, depending on who ends up on the roster. If we can expect the usual velocity uptick when a pitcher migrates to the bullpen, James has the potential to be a dynamic asset late in games in 2019.

YEAR	TEAM	LVL	AGE	WHIP	ERA	DRA	WARP	MPH	FB%	WHF	CSP
2016	LNC	A+	23	1.45	4.81	4.46	1.2				
2017	CCH	AA	24	1.46	4.38	3.59	1.3				
2018	CCH	AA	25	1.25	2.49	1.73	0.9				
2018	FRE	AAA	25	1.09	3.40	2.35	3.3				
2018	HOU	MLB	25	0.96	2.35	3.20	0.5	99.8	59.9	14.6	46.7
2019	HOU	MLB	26	1.23	3.39	3.82	1.6	99.4	61	14.9	47.5

Josh James, continued

Pitch Shape vs LHH

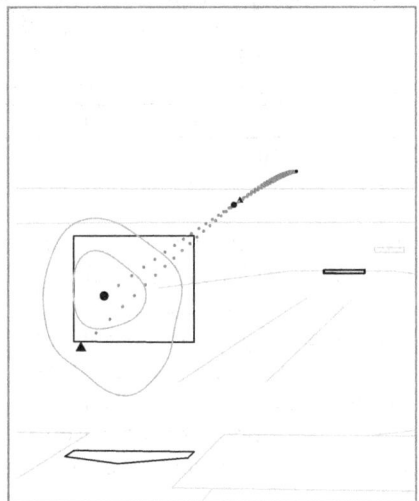

Pitch Shape vs RHH

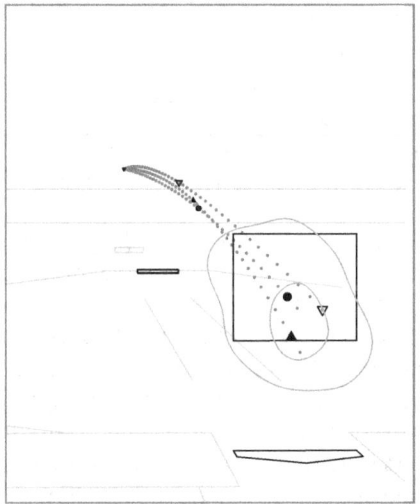

Type	Frequency	Velocity	H Movement	V Movement
● Fastball	59.9%	97.5 [116]	-11.3 [78]	-14 [106]
☐ Sinker				
+ Cutter				
▲ Changeup	23.2%	88.8 [114]	-14.8 [81]	-29.7 [93]
× Splitter				
▽ Slider	16.9%	85.5 [105]	7.7 [112]	-34.6 [95]
◇ Curveball				
✦ Slow Curveball				
✳ Knuckleball				
▼ Screwball				

Lance McCullers RHP

Born: 10/02/93   Age: 25   Bats: L   Throws: R
Height: 6'1"   Weight: 205   Origin: Round 1, 2012 Draft (#41 overall)

YEAR	TEAM	LVL	AGE	W	L	SV	G	GS	IP	H	HR	BB/9	K/9	K	GB%	BABIP
2016	HOU	MLB	22	6	5	0	14	14	81	80	5	5.0	11.8	106	59%	.383
2017	HOU	MLB	23	7	4	0	22	22	118²	114	8	3.0	10.0	132	62%	.330
2018	HOU	MLB	24	10	6	0	25	22	128¹	100	12	3.5	10.0	142	56%	.278
2019	HOU	MLB	25	8	5	0	20	20	110²	87	8	3.7	10.3	127	54%	.290

Breakout: 28%   Improve: 62%   Collapse: 15%   Attrition: 11%   MLB: 99%
Comparables: Chad Billingsley, Yovani Gallardo, Rich Harden

American poet laureate Lil Jon eloquently summed up McCullers's approach to pitching when he asserted that one should "Shake What [Their] Mama Gave [Them]." In this particular case, what his mama gave him was a dastardly curveball that he employed to strike out fools left and right. Not unlike Icarus, however, McCullers pushed his body to unsustainable limits that caused him to come crashing back down to Earth, having thrown so many curveballs that he broke his dang elbow. Tommy John surgery was performed in the offseason, and McCullers is expected to return in 2020. Sadly, this is yet another cautionary tale of a life torn asunder by Lil Jon.

YEAR	TEAM	LVL	AGE	WHIP	ERA	DRA	WARP	MPH	FB%	WHF	CSP
2016	HOU	MLB	22	1.54	3.22	3.65	1.6	97.0	43.2	13.7	43.4
2017	HOU	MLB	23	1.30	4.25	4.13	1.9	96.5	40.4	12.8	45.4
2018	HOU	MLB	24	1.17	3.86	3.30	3.0	96.3	37.4	14.3	43.9
2019	HOU	MLB	25	1.20	3.37	3.57	2.4	96.2	40.4	14	45.3

Lance McCullers, continued

Pitch Shape vs LHH

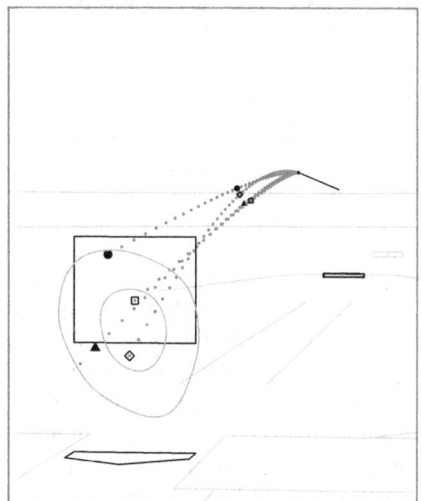

Pitch Shape vs RHH

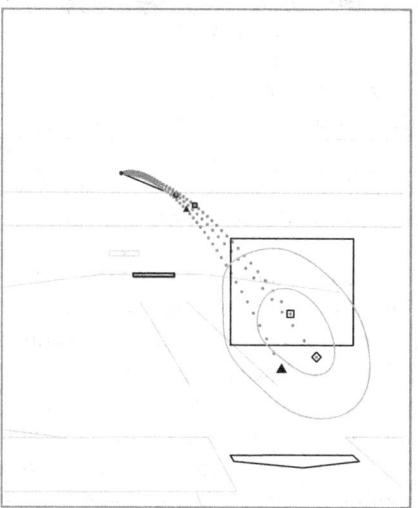

Type	Frequency	Velocity	H Movement	V Movement
● Fastball	3.2%	94.9 [108]	-8.5 [92]	-15.7 [100]
□ Sinker	33.8%	94.7 [111]	-13.5 [93]	-20.1 [101]
+ Cutter	0.3%	93.8 [130]	-2.3 [75]	-20.6 [113]
▲ Changeup	16.0%	87.7 [109]	-14.5 [83]	-30 [92]
✕ Splitter				
▽ Slider				
◇ Curveball	46.7%	86.2 [129]	7 [97]	-39.3 [120]
⊕ Slow Curveball				
✴ Knuckleball				
▼ Screwball				

Collin McHugh RHP

Born: 06/19/87 Age: 32 Bats: R Throws: R
Height: 6'2" Weight: 190 Origin: Round 18, 2008 Draft (#554 overall)

YEAR	TEAM	LVL	AGE	W	L	SV	G	GS	IP	H	HR	BB/9	K/9	K	GB%	BABIP
2016	HOU	MLB	29	13	10	0	33	33	184^2	206	25	2.6	8.6	177	43%	.339
2017	CCH	AA	30	0	0	0	4	4	15	18	1	2.4	6.6	11	57%	.340
2017	HOU	MLB	30	5	2	0	12	12	63^1	62	7	2.8	8.8	62	33%	.312
2018	HOU	MLB	31	6	2	0	58	0	72^1	45	6	2.6	11.7	94	35%	.248
2019	HOU	MLB	32	9	6	0	44	18	122	105	15	3.0	10.4	142	39%	.294

Breakout: 10% Improve: 33% Collapse: 29% Attrition: 11% MLB: 89%
Comparables: Jake Peavy, Kelvim Escobar, Johnny Cueto

It's probably safe to assume that McHugh has started his last game, at least for the Houston Astros. The usually-good-never-great starter couldn't find a spot in the rotation in 2018, so off to the bullpen he went. There, he found another two ticks on his fastball and a knack for striking out hitters at an unprecedented (for him) rate. It's generally a good sign when batters are swinging more at your pitches out of the strike zone and swinging less at the ones in, showing that he was getting more life on his pitches than just pure velocity in short work. He can double as both a long relief and high-leverage pitcher and will no doubt have his place in the bullpen cemented come 2019.

YEAR	TEAM	LVL	AGE	WHIP	ERA	DRA	WARP	MPH	FB%	WHF	CSP
2016	HOU	MLB	29	1.41	4.34	3.81	3.3	92.6	35.8	11.4	46.2
2017	CCH	AA	30	1.47	3.60	2.87	0.4				
2017	HOU	MLB	30	1.29	3.55	4.58	0.7	91.7	50.6	13.2	48.4
2018	HOU	MLB	31	0.91	1.99	2.70	1.9	93.5	49.6	14.1	47.1
2019	HOU	MLB	32	1.19	3.59	3.99	2.0	91.8	42.8	12.5	46.9

Collin McHugh, continued

Pitch Shape vs LHH

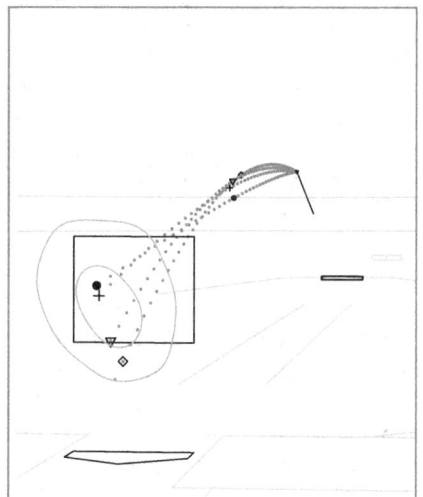

Pitch Shape vs RHH

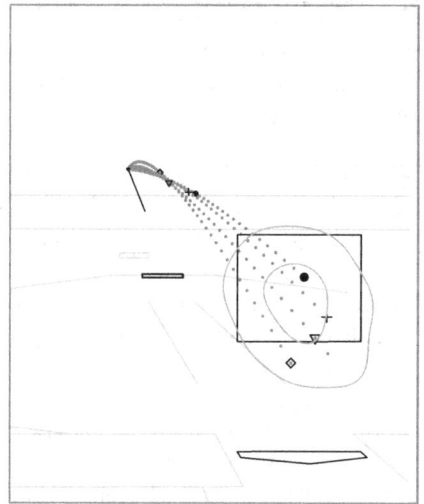

Type	Frequency	Velocity	H Movement	V Movement
● Fastball	49.5%	92.5 [100]	-7.5 [96]	-14.5 [104]
□ Sinker	0.1%	91.7 [96]	-12.6 [100]	-23.6 [89]
+ Cutter	8.1%	88.1 [96]	3.7 [110]	-26.5 [89]
▲ Changeup	0.3%	87.1 [107]	-11.5 [99]	-26.5 [102]
× Splitter				
▽ Slider	24.1%	80 [80]	15.7 [147]	-41.5 [75]
◇ Curveball	17.9%	76.2 [92]	12.1 [118]	-55.1 [84]
⊕ Slow Curveball	0.1%	69.1 [103]	10.8 [101]	-67.5 [99]
✳ Knuckleball				
▼ Screwball				

Wade Miley   LHP

Born: 11/13/86   Age: 32   Bats: L   Throws: L
Height: 6'0"   Weight: 220   Origin: Round 1, 2008 Draft (#43 overall)

YEAR	TEAM	LVL	AGE	W	L	SV	G	GS	IP	H	HR	BB/9	K/9	K	GB%	BABIP
2016	SEA	MLB	29	7	8	0	19	19	112	117	18	2.7	6.6	82	48%	.298
2016	BAL	MLB	29	2	5	0	11	11	54	70	7	2.5	9.2	55	50%	.389
2017	BAL	MLB	30	8	15	0	32	32	157^1	179	25	5.3	8.1	142	51%	.332
2018	BLX	AA	31	1	2	0	7	7	25^1	27	3	1.4	9.9	28	59%	.393
2018	MIL	MLB	31	5	2	0	16	16	80^2	71	3	3.0	5.6	50	54%	.269
2019	HOU	MLB	32	7	5	0	19	19	95	98	12	3.4	7.2	76	50%	.299

Breakout: 15%   Improve: 46%   Collapse: 24%   Attrition: 17%   MLB: 86%
Comparables: Gavin Floyd, Paul Maholm, Tom Koehler

Revitalize your career in 10 steps: Cutter. Cutter. Change. Cutter. Curve. Cutter. Fastball. Curve. Cutter. Change. Miley deserves this pitch selection shoutout, as the struggling southpaw allegedly decided to throw cutters in the middle of a July 25, 2017 start against Tampa Bay because he was getting shelled. After that fateful decision, this veritable Paul Bunyan became a minor-league wizard for the Brewers, and dodged a couple of injuries to become a near-ace for the surprise contenders. The Legend of Wade Miley shows the tantalizing appeal of baseball's game of adjustments, but there's danger in merely leaning on the crutch of "learn a new pitch." Plus, it takes credit away from the difficulty of Miley's path: learn a new pitch, execute that pitch, take a minor-league contract, work in the minors, improve command, rehab injuries and throw that newfound pitch more and more as the season progresses. It only looks easy when it works. This one's a true legend for being so much more than a myth.

YEAR	TEAM	LVL	AGE	WHIP	ERA	DRA	WARP	MPH	FB%	WHF	CSP
2016	SEA	MLB	29	1.35	4.98	5.11	0.3	93.3	47	9.4	47.3
2016	BAL	MLB	29	1.57	6.17	4.06	0.8	92.8	47	9.8	42.6
2017	BAL	MLB	30	1.73	5.61	7.20	-2.9	93.3	53.4	9	36.9
2018	BLX	AA	31	1.22	3.55	3.61	0.5				
2018	MIL	MLB	31	1.21	2.57	4.13	1.1	92.6	20	9.9	42.5
2019	HOU	MLB	32	1.43	4.49	4.96	0.5	92.1	43	9.3	41

Wade Miley, continued

Pitch Shape vs LHH

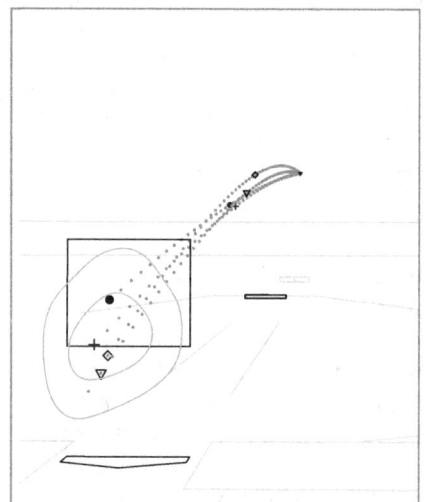

Pitch Shape vs RHH

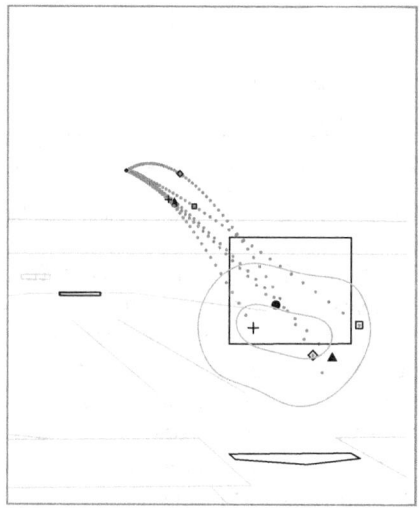

Type		Frequency	Velocity	H Movement	V Movement
●	Fastball	11.4%	91.8 [98]	4.4 [111]	-14.1 [105]
□	Sinker	8.6%	90.6 [91]	10.9 [114]	-17.1 [111]
+	Cutter	42.0%	88.1 [96]	-1.4 [97]	-24.1 [98]
▲	Changeup	16.7%	82.9 [90]	13.5 [88]	-26.5 [102]
×	Splitter				
▽	Slider	4.5%	80.6 [83]	-3.9 [96]	-43.2 [70]
◇	Curveball	16.8%	75.8 [90]	-5.7 [91]	-54 [87]
⊕	Slow Curveball				
✽	Knuckleball				
▼	Screwball				

Roberto Osuna RHP

Born: 02/07/95   Age: 24   Bats: R   Throws: R
Height: 6'2"   Weight: 215   Origin: International Free Agent, 2011

YEAR	TEAM	LVL	AGE	W	L	SV	G	GS	IP	H	HR	BB/9	K/9	K	GB%	BABIP
2016	TOR	MLB	21	4	3	36	72	0	74	55	9	1.7	10.0	82	35%	.256
2017	TOR	MLB	22	3	4	39	66	0	64	46	3	1.3	11.7	83	47%	.285
2018	TOR	MLB	23	0	0	9	15	0	15^1	16	0	0.6	7.6	13	40%	.340
2018	HOU	MLB	23	2	2	12	23	0	22^2	17	1	1.2	7.5	19	44%	.258
2019	HOU	MLB	24	3	2	35	52	0	54	48	6	2.8	9.3	57	41%	.285

Breakout: 31%   Improve: 51%   Collapse: 12%   Attrition: 10%   MLB: 97%
Comparables: Huston Street, Joakim Soria, Drew Storen

On May 8th, Osuna was arrested in Toronto on assault charges. Details remain mostly sealed, but the victim was the mother of Osuna's child, and he later reached a plea agreement that included a peace bond and no contact order. After six weeks on administrative leave, Osuna and Major League Baseball ultimately agreed that he would serve a 75-game suspension under the Joint Domestic Violence, Sexual Assault and Child Abuse policy, the second-longest suspension administered under the policy since its implementation in 2015. The Astros traded for the still-suspended Osuna at the deadline, sending banished former closer Ken Giles and two prospects to Toronto. General Manager Jeff Luhnow repeatedly defended acquiring Osuna, citing the team's "culture" and Osuna's "remorse," while sidestepping a claimed organizational "zero-tolerance" policy for domestic abuse. The suspension had the perverse effect of making Osuna a more valuable asset to a team morally bankrupt enough to profit off domestic violence: The Astros gained an extra year of control since players under suspension don't accrue service time, and despite the suspension he was eligible to pitch for his new team in the playoffs. Baseball needs to be better than this.

YEAR	TEAM	LVL	AGE	WHIP	ERA	DRA	WARP	MPH	FB%	WHF	CSP
2016	TOR	MLB	21	0.93	2.68	3.12	1.6	98.3	66.3	16.6	48.5
2017	TOR	MLB	22	0.86	3.38	2.41	2.0	95.9	48	17.6	41.9
2018	TOR	MLB	23	1.11	2.93	3.97	0.2	97.1	47.4	13.4	50.5
2018	HOU	MLB	23	0.88	1.99	3.54	0.4	96.6	47.4	16.9	48.3
2019	HOU	MLB	24	1.17	3.53	3.99	0.7	96.8	55.7	17.2	48

Roberto Osuna, continued

Pitch Shape vs LHH

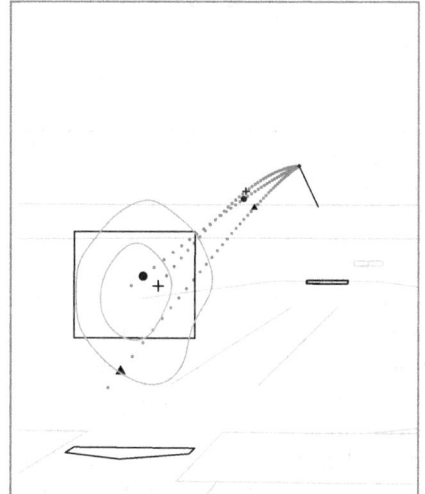

Pitch Shape vs RHH

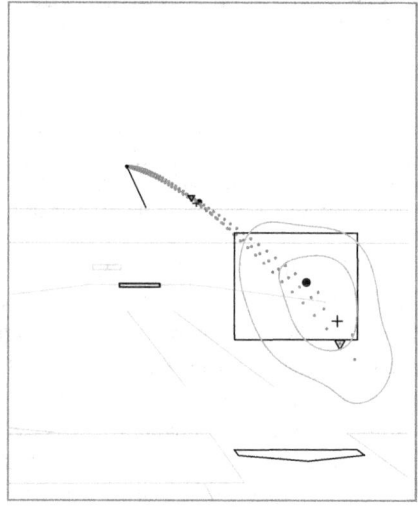

Type	Frequency	Velocity	H Movement	V Movement
● Fastball	50.3%	95.7 [110]	-4.9 [108]	-10.3 [117]
□ Sinker	5.6%	95.3 [114]	-11 [113]	-13.1 [124]
+ Cutter	21.5%	91.1 [114]	5.1 [119]	-19.5 [117]
▲ Changeup	9.4%	83.6 [93]	-11.4 [99]	-24.2 [109]
× Splitter				
▽ Slider	13.2%	86.9 [111]	6.3 [106]	-31 [106]
◇ Curveball				
✥ Slow Curveball				
✳ Knuckleball				
▼ Screwball				

Brad Peacock   RHP
Born: 02/02/88   Age: 31   Bats: R   Throws: R
Height: 6'1"   Weight: 210   Origin: Round 41, 2006 Draft (#1231 overall)

YEAR	TEAM	LVL	AGE	W	L	SV	G	GS	IP	H	HR	BB/9	K/9	K	GB%	BABIP
2016	FRE	AAA	28	5	6	0	22	21	117	122	11	3.1	9.2	119	44%	.335
2016	HOU	MLB	28	0	1	0	10	5	31^2	21	6	4.0	8.0	28	41%	.190
2017	HOU	MLB	29	13	2	0	34	21	132	100	10	3.9	11.0	161	44%	.286
2018	HOU	MLB	30	3	5	3	61	1	65	56	11	2.8	13.3	96	37%	.317
2019	HOU	MLB	31	5	4	0	58	6	84	66	8	3.3	11.1	105	40%	.287

Breakout: 34%   Improve: 64%   Collapse: 19%   Attrition: 16%   MLB: 95%
Comparables: Glen Perkins, Juan Nicasio, Tom Gorzelanny

Much like Colin McHugh, it would seem as if Peacock's days as a starting pitcher are over. It's certainly not for a lack of chances, but history has seemed to prove that Peacock just doesn't have the longevity to last much farther than a run or two through the order. That will probably sit nicely with Houston, however, as his transition to the 'pen led to a drastic increase his strikeout rate and a significant drop in his walk rate. His overall durability doesn't seem to be an issue, either, as he was tied for the second-most games pitched on the team with 61. The promising starter who never quite produced has a new home in the Houston bullpen. In the past, this was seen as a demotion. In this new age of baseball, it's simply a new lease on life.

YEAR	TEAM	LVL	AGE	WHIP	ERA	DRA	WARP	MPH	FB%	WHF	CSP
2016	FRE	AAA	28	1.38	4.23	3.32	2.7				
2016	HOU	MLB	28	1.11	3.69	4.84	0.2	94.1	52.6	8.7	49.7
2017	HOU	MLB	29	1.19	3.00	2.91	3.8	93.9	51.3	12.9	47.8
2018	HOU	MLB	30	1.17	3.46	2.54	1.8	94.6	54.6	13.9	45.4
2019	HOU	MLB	31	1.14	3.08	3.54	1.7	93.3	52.3	12.8	47

Brad Peacock, continued

Pitch Shape vs LHH

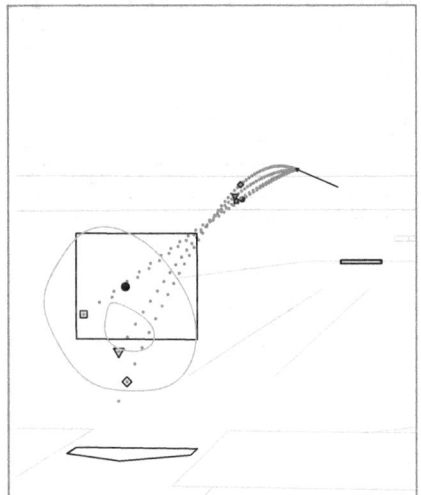

Pitch Shape vs RHH

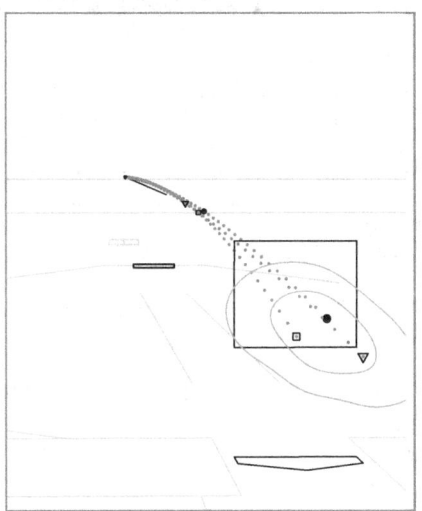

Type	Frequency	Velocity	H Movement	V Movement
● Fastball	26.0%	93.4 [103]	-9.9 [85]	-15.1 [102]
□ Sinker	28.6%	92.8 [102]	-15.2 [78]	-21.1 [97]
+ Cutter				
▲ Changeup	0.8%	83.5 [93]	-12.2 [95]	-28.3 [97]
× Splitter				
▽ Slider	40.2%	82.5 [91]	11.3 [128]	-29.7 [110]
◇ Curveball	4.4%	78.9 [102]	11 [113]	-51.1 [93]
⊕ Slow Curveball				
✳ Knuckleball				
▼ Screwball				

Cionel Perez LHP

Born: 04/21/96 Age: 23 Bats: L Throws: L
Height: 5'11" Weight: 170 Origin: International Free Agent, 2016

YEAR	TEAM	LVL	AGE	W	L	SV	G	GS	IP	H	HR	BB/9	K/9	K	GB%	BABIP
2017	QUD	A	21	4	3	2	12	9	55¹	52	2	2.8	8.9	55	51%	.331
2017	BCA	A+	21	2	1	0	5	4	25¹	27	1	1.8	6.4	18	46%	.325
2017	CCH	AA	21	0	0	0	4	3	13	15	1	3.5	6.9	10	33%	.341
2018	CCH	AA	22	6	1	1	16	11	68¹	54	3	2.9	10.9	83	47%	.304
2018	HOU	MLB	22	0	0	0	8	0	11¹	6	3	5.6	9.5	12	58%	.130
2019	HOU	MLB	23	4	3	0	36	5	57	50	6	3.6	9.5	61	44%	.291

Breakout: 10% Improve: 14% Collapse: 7% Attrition: 14% MLB: 29%
Comparables: Matt Bowman, Buddy Baumann, Gio Gonzalez

INTERIOR: *A kitchen in a middle-class home. A teenager enters and drops her backpack on the kitchen table.*

Mother: Hi Honey! How was school today?
Daughter: Fine.
Mother: Fine?
Daughter: Yep.
Mother: Just fine? Nothing interesting happened?
Daughter: No, Mom. I'd say my day was analogous to the pitching career of Houston prospect Cionel Perez. While nothing overtly promising developed, it also shouldn't be characterized as a failure or disappointment. It was ... fine. That is the most robust word that could be used to describe my day.
Mother: I don't like your tone.
Daughter: Well, I'm not crazy about Cionel Perez's walk rate during his admittedly short stint with the 2018 Astros. Yet, here we are. We cope.

YEAR	TEAM	LVL	AGE	WHIP	ERA	DRA	WARP	MPH	FB%	WHF	CSP
2017	QUD	A	21	1.25	4.39	3.65	1.0				
2017	BCA	A+	21	1.26	2.84	3.58	0.5				
2017	CCH	AA	21	1.54	5.54	3.51	0.2				
2018	CCH	AA	22	1.11	1.98	3.08	1.7				
2018	HOU	MLB	22	1.15	3.97	4.58	0.0	96.9	63.2	11.8	41.6
2019	HOU	MLB	23	1.26	3.68	4.08	0.8	96.8	65.5	12.2	43.1

Cionel Perez, continued

Pitch Shape vs LHH

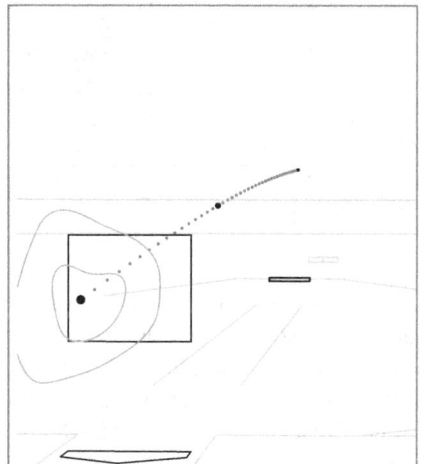

Pitch Shape vs RHH

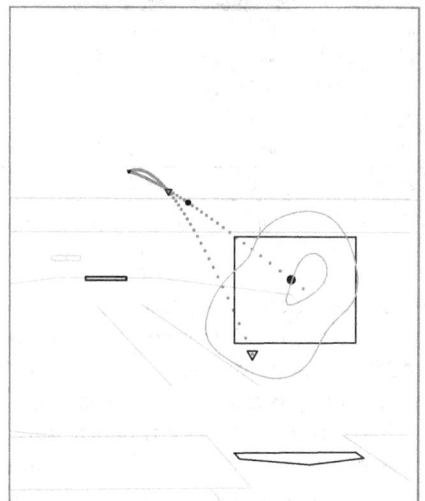

Type	Frequency	Velocity	H Movement	V Movement
● Fastball	63.2%	95.6 [110]	3.5 [114]	-11.4 [114]
☐ Sinker				
+ Cutter				
▲ Changeup	6.8%	87.9 [110]	14.3 [84]	-22.8 [113]
✕ Splitter				
▽ Slider	28.2%	84.8 [102]	-2.4 [89]	-37.7 [86]
◇ Curveball	1.8%	80.2 [106]	-6.7 [95]	-52.5 [90]
✥ Slow Curveball				
✱ Knuckleball				
▼ Screwball				

Astros Player Analysis - 67

Ryan Pressly RHP

Born: 12/15/88 Age: 30 Bats: R Throws: R
Height: 6'3" Weight: 210 Origin: Round 11, 2007 Draft (#354 overall)

YEAR	TEAM	LVL	AGE	W	L	SV	G	GS	IP	H	HR	BB/9	K/9	K	GB%	BABIP
2016	MIN	MLB	27	6	7	1	72	0	75^1	79	8	2.7	8.0	67	41%	.311
2017	ROC	AAA	28	2	0	4	7	0	10	5	0	4.5	13.5	15	55%	.250
2017	MIN	MLB	28	2	3	0	57	0	61^1	52	10	2.8	9.0	61	52%	.264
2018	MIN	MLB	29	1	1	0	51	0	47^2	46	5	3.6	13.0	69	50%	.363
2018	HOU	MLB	29	1	0	2	26	0	23^1	11	1	1.2	12.3	32	62%	.213
2019	HOU	MLB	30	3	2	5	57	0	60^1	47	5	3.3	11.0	74	48%	.290

Breakout: 32% Improve: 55% Collapse: 18% Attrition: 15% MLB: 90%
Comparables: Jason Frasor, Xavier Cedeno, Kevin Jepsen

If you want definitive proof that saves are dead from an analytical standpoint, here you go. The Astros sent two prospects to Minnesota for Pressly's services, and it wasn't hard to see why when he landed in Houston. The long-time setup man honed his craft over the years, building up velocity and increasing the spin on his pitches, until he ultimately transformed himself into one of the best relievers in the game. Free from Minnesota's subpar overall defense, Pressly's numbers rose to meet his peripherals in spectacular fashion. He still has one more year of arbitration eligibility left, so expect Houston to utilize him and his extremely nasty slider as much as they can in 2019.

YEAR	TEAM	LVL	AGE	WHIP	ERA	DRA	WARP	MPH	FB%	WHF	CSP
2016	MIN	MLB	27	1.35	3.70	3.90	0.9	98.0	54	12.3	47.6
2017	ROC	AAA	28	1.00	0.90	1.39	0.4				
2017	MIN	MLB	28	1.16	4.70	3.48	1.2	97.8	55	13.4	49.4
2018	MIN	MLB	29	1.36	3.40	1.97	1.6	97.7	48.6	19.4	47.2
2018	HOU	MLB	29	0.60	0.77	1.73	0.9	97.5	34.7	17.7	47.6
2019	HOU	MLB	30	1.15	2.84	3.34	1.3	97.0	50.1	15.4	47.9

Ryan Pressly, continued

Pitch Shape vs LHH

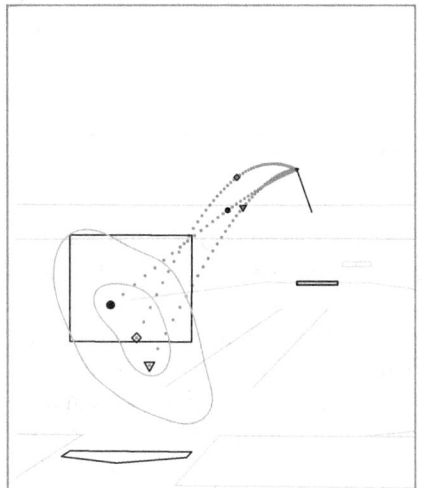

Pitch Shape vs RHH

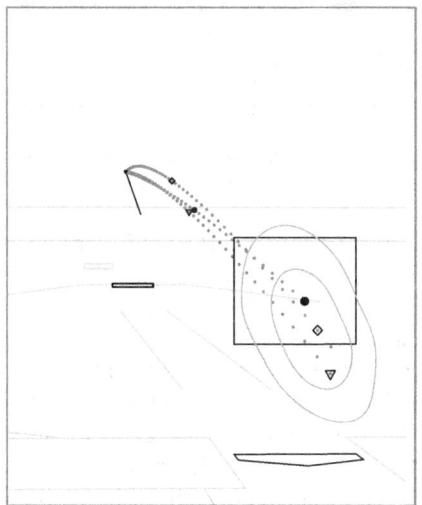

Type	Frequency	Velocity	H Movement	V Movement
● Fastball	41.1%	96.3 [112]	-1.2 [125]	-11.6 [113]
☐ Sinker	3.5%	94.8 [112]	-10.5 [117]	-18.4 [106]
+ Cutter				
▲ Changeup				
✕ Splitter				
▽ Slider	27.3%	90.1 [125]	5.4 [102]	-29.5 [110]
◇ Curveball	28.1%	83.3 [118]	15.3 [131]	-46.1 [104]
✪ Slow Curveball				
✱ Knuckleball				
▼ Screwball				

Astros Player Analysis - 69

Hector Rondon RHP

Born: 02/26/88　Age: 31　Bats: R　Throws: R
Height: 6'3"　Weight: 230　Origin: International Free Agent, 2004

YEAR	TEAM	LVL	AGE	W	L	SV	G	GS	IP	H	HR	BB/9	K/9	K	GB%	BABIP
2016	CHN	MLB	28	2	3	18	54	0	51	42	8	1.4	10.2	58	49%	.274
2017	CHN	MLB	29	4	1	0	61	0	57¹	50	10	3.1	10.8	69	48%	.292
2018	HOU	MLB	30	2	5	15	63	0	59	58	4	3.1	10.2	67	48%	.340
2019	*HOU*	*MLB*	*31*	*3*	*2*	*5*	*52*	*0*	*54*	*48*	*7*	*3.1*	*9.7*	*59*	*47%*	*.289*

Breakout: 28%　Improve: 43%　Collapse: 27%　Attrition: 7%　MLB: 89%
Comparables: Greg McMichael, Bobby Jenks, Joakim Soria

Former Cubs stalwart Hector Rondon was yet another addition for the 2018 Astros, a team desperate to address some surprising letdowns in their bullpen (or one with nothing else left to improve). Fallen from grace in Chicago, the Astros used him to bridge the gap between Giles and Osuna, and he turned in one of his better seasons to date despite battling some unlucky BABIP numbers. He'll be 31 as he plays the last of his two-year deal in 2019, and has shown no signs of stopping—even seeing an uptick in fastball velocity last season. Roster shuffling is always a factor, but Rondon should be in line to continue acting as a high-leverage reliever in the immediate future.

YEAR	TEAM	LVL	AGE	WHIP	ERA	DRA	WARP	MPH	FB%	WHF	CSP
2016	CHN	MLB	28	0.98	3.53	2.52	1.4	98.5	63.3	11.7	50.1
2017	CHN	MLB	29	1.22	4.24	3.29	1.2	98.3	61.6	13	47.7
2018	HOU	MLB	30	1.32	3.20	2.81	1.4	98.8	61.7	14.7	48.9
2019	*HOU*	*MLB*	*31*	*1.22*	*3.61*	*4.04*	*0.7*	*97.7*	*61.6*	*13.4*	*48.5*

Hector Rondon, continued

Pitch Shape vs LHH

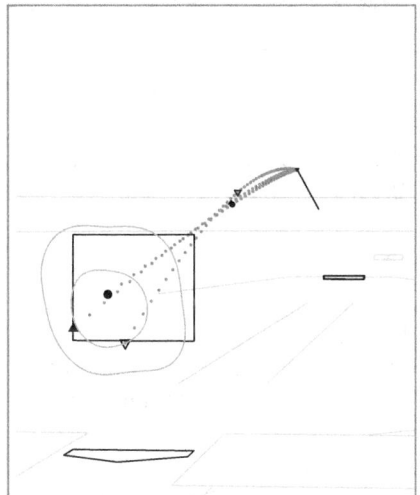

Pitch Shape vs RHH

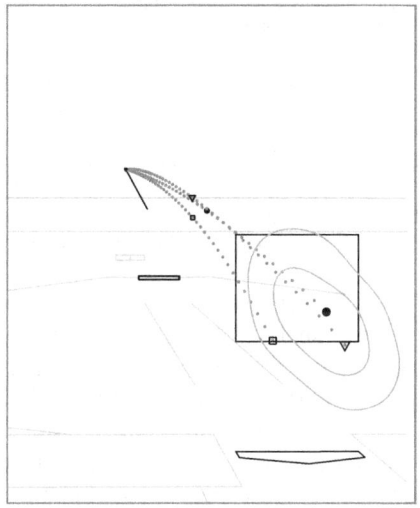

Type	Frequency	Velocity	H Movement	V Movement
● Fastball	56.4%	97.6 [116]	-7 [99]	-12.7 [110]
□ Sinker	5.3%	97.6 [125]	-13 [97]	-16.7 [112]
+ Cutter				
▲ Changeup	4.3%	92 [126]	-14.4 [83]	-25 [107]
× Splitter				
▽ Slider	34.0%	87.1 [112]	5.8 [104]	-32.8 [101]
◇ Curveball				
⊕ Slow Curveball				
✳ Knuckleball				
▼ Screwball				

Joe Smith RHP

Born: 03/22/84   Age: 35   Bats: R   Throws: R
Height: 6'2"   Weight: 205   Origin: Round 3, 2006 Draft (#94 overall)

YEAR	TEAM	LVL	AGE	W	L	SV	G	GS	IP	H	HR	BB/9	K/9	K	GB%	BABIP
2016	ANA	MLB	32	1	4	6	38	0	37^2	36	4	3.1	6.0	25	57%	.283
2016	CHN	MLB	32	1	1	0	16	0	14^1	11	4	3.1	9.4	15	36%	.219
2017	TOR	MLB	33	3	0	0	38	0	35^2	30	3	2.5	12.9	51	44%	.342
2017	CLE	MLB	33	0	0	1	21	0	18^1	16	1	0.0	9.8	20	60%	.306
2018	HOU	MLB	34	5	1	0	56	0	45^2	34	7	2.4	9.1	46	45%	.239
2019	HOU	MLB	35	1	0	0	10	0	11	10	1	3.4	9.0	11	47%	.290

Breakout: 24%   Improve: 43%   Collapse: 25%   Attrition: 11%   MLB: 87%
Comparables: Akinori Otsuka, Scott Downs, Scott Eyre

Joe Smith parlayed his penchant for embarrassing right-handed hitters into a two-year deal with Houston before the 2018 season. While it's unfair to say he regressed in 2018, in the sense that 2017 was probably the outlier, he didn't find the same successes due to a pretty significant dip in his strikeout rate and a bump in home run rate against righties. He did make the ALCS roster, which given the Astros' bullpen depth, is an achievement unto itself. If Smith can do some minor tweaking, he should bounce back as the righty-killer Houston hoped he'd be in 2019.

YEAR	TEAM	LVL	AGE	WHIP	ERA	DRA	WARP	MPH	FB%	WHF	CSP
2016	ANA	MLB	32	1.30	3.82	6.86	-0.8	90.6	63.5	9.2	44.8
2016	CHN	MLB	32	1.12	2.51	6.18	-0.2	90.6	57.8	9.4	47.7
2017	TOR	MLB	33	1.12	3.28	3.28	0.8	90.6	67.7	13.4	52.8
2017	CLE	MLB	33	0.87	3.44	3.54	0.3	90.1	64.2	10.6	53.2
2018	HOU	MLB	34	1.01	3.74	4.49	0.2	89.4	65.1	11.2	50.5
2019	HOU	MLB	35	1.26	4.05	4.42	0.1	88.9	63.6	10.9	49.2

Joe Smith, continued

Pitch Shape vs LHH

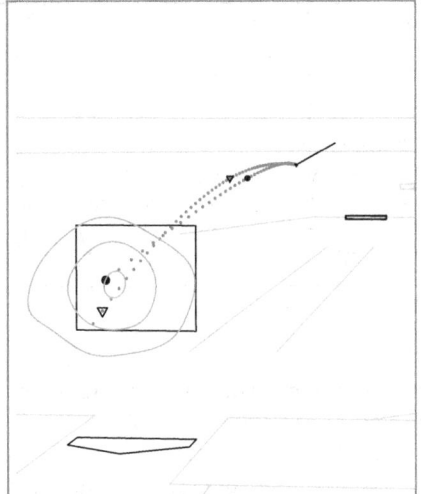

Pitch Shape vs RHH

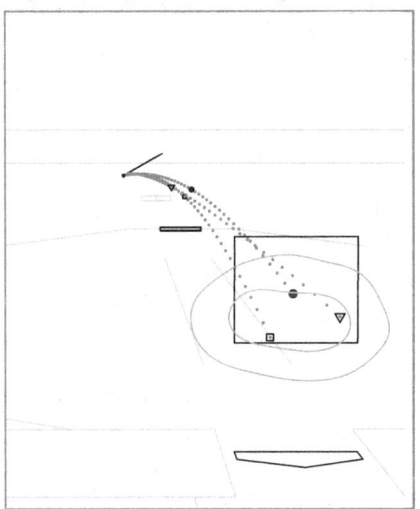

Type	Frequency	Velocity	H Movement	V Movement
● Fastball	32.0%	88.6 [87]	-15.3 [60]	-26.6 [66]
□ Sinker	33.0%	87.9 [77]	-15.6 [75]	-35.3 [51]
+ Cutter				
▲ Changeup	0.3%	79.5 [77]	-13.6 [87]	-41.8 [57]
× Splitter				
▽ Slider	34.6%	79.1 [76]	13.9 [139]	-31.7 [104]
◇ Curveball				
⊕ Slow Curveball				
✳ Knuckleball				
▼ Screwball				

Astros Player Analysis - 73

Framber Valdez LHP

Born: 11/19/93 Age: 25 Bats: L Throws: L
Height: 5'11" Weight: 170 Origin: International Free Agent, 2015

YEAR	TEAM	LVL	AGE	W	L	SV	G	GS	IP	H	HR	BB/9	K/9	K	GB%	BABIP
2016	GRV	RK	22	1	0	0	2	2	10^2	7	0	2.5	12.7	15	79%	.292
2016	TCV	A-	22	2	1	0	5	2	21^2	22	0	2.9	11.6	28	78%	.379
2016	QUD	A	22	1	3	0	6	6	35^1	31	1	2.8	8.9	35	65%	.316
2017	BCA	A+	23	2	3	1	13	9	61^1	41	3	4.3	10.7	73	57%	.257
2017	CCH	AA	23	5	5	0	12	9	49	60	4	4.2	9.7	53	60%	.394
2018	CCH	AA	24	4	5	1	20	13	94^1	92	7	2.8	11.4	120	58%	.363
2018	FRE	AAA	24	2	0	0	2	1	8^2	8	0	3.1	9.3	9	48%	.348
2018	HOU	MLB	24	4	1	0	8	5	37	22	3	5.8	8.3	34	71%	.213
2019	HOU	MLB	25	5	3	0	18	13	70	64	7	3.9	9.3	73	54%	.298

Breakout: 18%   Improve: 34%   Collapse: 24%   Attrition: 34%   MLB: 68%
Comparables: Jeremy Jeffress, Luke Jackson, Enny Romero

He's a short, beefy groundballin' lefty named Framber. (The listed weight might be, uh, a little light here.) Suffice to say, he's going to be a popular player for irony's sake if nothing else, but he's got a shot to be more than that. Valdez didn't make his pro debut until he was 21, downright ancient for a signing out of the Dominican, and is a testament to Houston knocking down every door to acquire talent. He got a lot of outs down the stretch for the Astros in a swingman role, although his characteristically good command deserted him and thus the rest of his line doesn't match the pretty ERA. The urge to make him a LOOGY as a small sinker/curveball lefty will be strong; that urge could limit a higher ceiling.

YEAR	TEAM	LVL	AGE	WHIP	ERA	DRA	WARP	MPH	FB%	WHF	CSP
2016	GRV	RK	22	0.94	1.69	1.41	0.5				
2016	TCV	A-	22	1.34	3.74	2.99	0.5				
2016	QUD	A	22	1.19	3.06	4.40	0.3				
2017	BCA	A+	23	1.14	2.79	3.54	1.2				
2017	CCH	AA	23	1.69	5.88	4.12	0.6				
2018	CCH	AA	24	1.28	4.10	3.58	1.8				
2018	FRE	AAA	24	1.27	4.15	4.16	0.1				
2018	HOU	MLB	24	1.24	2.19	6.12	-0.4	94.3	69	8.9	43.9
2019	HOU	MLB	25	1.35	3.84	4.22	1.0	94.0	70.7	9.1	44.9

Framber Valdez, continued

Pitch Shape vs LHH

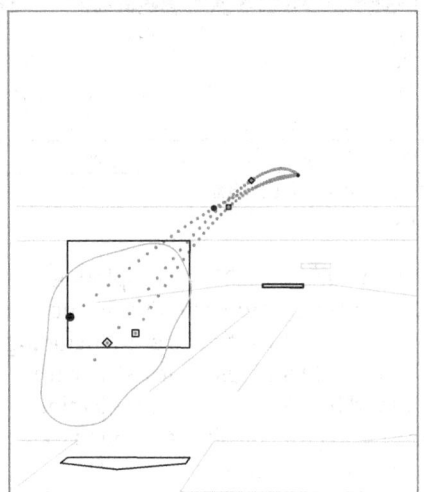

Pitch Shape vs RHH

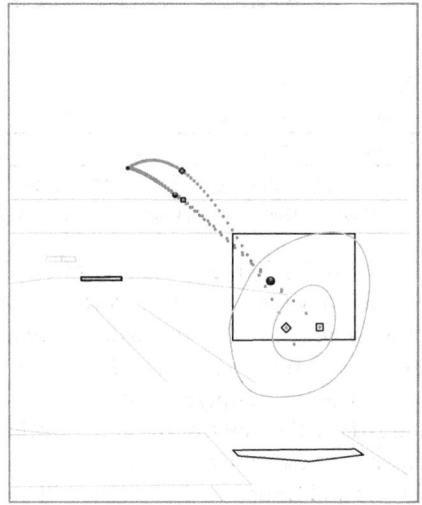

Type	Frequency	Velocity	H Movement	V Movement
● Fastball	23.9%	93.1 [102]	5.8 [104]	-16.5 [98]
□ Sinker	45.2%	92 [97]	13.8 [90]	-26.8 [79]
+ Cutter				
▲ Changeup	0.8%	86.6 [105]	12.5 [94]	-33.7 [81]
× Splitter				
▽ Slider				
◇ Curveball	30.2%	80.1 [106]	-10.5 [111]	-50.7 [94]
⊕ Slow Curveball				
✳ Knuckleball				
▼ Screwball				

Justin Verlander RHP

Born: 02/20/83   Age: 36   Bats: R   Throws: R
Height: 6'5"   Weight: 225   Origin: Round 1, 2004 Draft (#2 overall)

YEAR	TEAM	LVL	AGE	W	L	SV	G	GS	IP	H	HR	BB/9	K/9	K	GB%	BABIP
2016	DET	MLB	33	16	9	0	34	34	227^2	171	30	2.3	10.0	254	35%	.255
2017	DET	MLB	34	10	8	0	28	28	172	153	23	3.5	9.2	176	34%	.283
2017	HOU	MLB	34	5	0	0	5	5	34	17	4	1.3	11.4	43	32%	.194
2018	HOU	MLB	35	16	9	0	34	34	214	156	28	1.6	12.2	290	31%	.272
2019	HOU	MLB	36	15	8	0	30	30	189	155	27	2.5	10.8	227	34%	.283

Breakout: 15%   Improve: 38%   Collapse: 26%   Attrition: 10%   MLB: 88%
Comparables: Jason Schmidt, Chris Carpenter, David Cone

The Astros traded for Verlander at 11:59 PM on August 31, 2017, completing the deal literally two seconds before that season's waiver trade deadline. It's now pretty safe to say that one will go down as one of the best trades ever. Including two playoff runs, he's pitched to a 2.41 ERA over 302 innings as an Astro, with 388 strikeouts to only 58 walks. He's also added his seventh All-Star selection, the 2017 ALCS MVP trophy, and a World Series ring to a trophy case that already had a MVP, Cy Young, and Rookie of the Year from his Tigers days. He's Detroit's legend and Houston's hero, but he'll belong to Cooperstown six summers after he retires.

YEAR	TEAM	LVL	AGE	WHIP	ERA	DRA	WARP	MPH	FB%	WHF	CSP
2016	DET	MLB	33	1.00	3.04	3.40	5.1	96.8	57.3	13.4	45.8
2017	DET	MLB	34	1.28	3.82	4.03	3.0	97.3	58	11	47.8
2017	HOU	MLB	34	0.65	1.06	3.08	0.9	97.2	59.6	15.1	49.9
2018	HOU	MLB	35	0.90	2.52	2.33	7.3	97.1	61.2	16.2	51.6
2019	HOU	MLB	36	1.08	3.54	3.90	3.3	95.7	57.9	13.7	48

Justin Verlander, continued

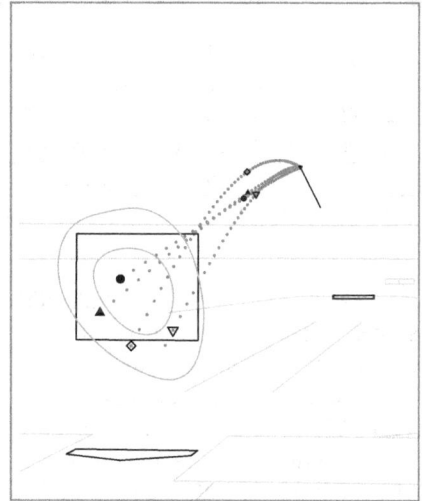
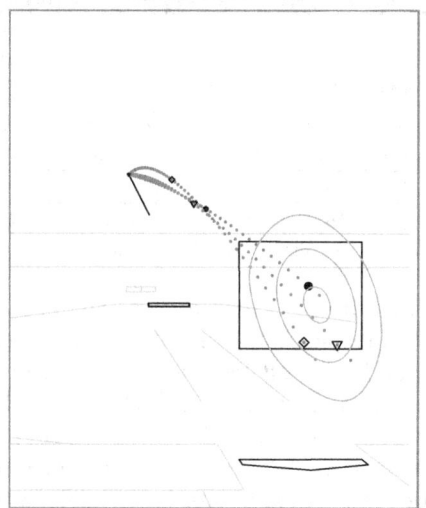

Type	Frequency	Velocity	H Movement	V Movement
● Fastball	61.2%	95.4 [109]	-9.2 [89]	-9.8 [119]
☐ Sinker				
+ Cutter	0.5%	92 [119]	-1.8 [78]	-18 [123]
▲ Changeup	1.5%	87.8 [110]	-14.3 [84]	-24.5 [108]
✕ Splitter				
▽ Slider	22.3%	86.8 [111]	3.6 [95]	-30.1 [109]
◇ Curveball	14.4%	79.8 [105]	8.6 [103]	-50.2 [95]
✥ Slow Curveball				
✳ Knuckleball				
▼ Screwball				

Houston Astros 2019

Yordan Alvarez LF

Born: 06/27/97   Age: 22   Bats: L   Throws: R
Height: 6'5"   Weight: 225   Origin: International Free Agent, 2016

YEAR	TEAM	LVL	AGE	PA	R	2B	3B	HR	RBI	BB	K	SB	CS	AVG/OBP/SLG
2016	DAR	ROK	19	57	7	2	1	1	4	12	7	2	1	.341/.474/.500
2017	QUD	A	20	139	26	6	0	9	33	23	36	2	0	.360/.468/.658
2017	BCA	A+	20	252	19	11	3	3	36	19	41	6	1	.277/.329/.393
2018	CCH	AA	21	190	39	13	0	12	46	19	45	5	2	.325/.389/.615
2018	FRE	AAA	21	189	24	8	0	8	28	23	47	1	0	.259/.349/.452
2019	HOU	MLB	22	62	8	3	0	3	8	5	19	0	0	.232/.295/.446

Breakout: 16%   Improve: 45%   Collapse: 1%   Attrition: 13%   MLB: 52%
Comparables: Thomas Neal, Clint Frazier, Jesse Winker

The Astros play the One Red Paperclip game as well as anyone in baseball. With the first pick in the 2012 Rule 5 Draft, Houston selected reliever/former first-rounder/castoff Josh Fields from the Red Sox. There he found a measure of control to go along with his fastball and knuckle curve, but Boston didn't protect him on the 40-man. Fields spent the next few years in the Houston bullpen, sometimes dominating and often underperforming. Meanwhile, the Dodgers signed Alvarez for $2 million out of Cuba late in the 2015-16 signing period. They quickly flipped him to the Astros for Fields, before Alvarez even made his American pro debut. While Fields has pitched very well in Los Angeles, the real prize here turned out to be Alvarez, now one of baseball's best hitting prospects. Not bad for the $50,000 Rule 5 price and six years of careful work.

YEAR	TEAM	LVL	AGE	PA	DRC+	VORP	BABIP	BRR	FRAA	WARP
2016	DAR	ROK	19	57	174	8.1	.378	0.1		0.4
2017	QUD	A	20	139	189	18.2	.449	-1.6	LF(13): -1.5, 1B(7): 0.0	1.1
2017	BCA	A+	20	252	116	7.2	.316	-0.2	LF(28): 2.6, 1B(15): -0.4	0.5
2018	CCH	AA	21	190	164	21.5	.377	0.2	LF(31): 3.6, 1B(5): -0.1	1.6
2018	FRE	AAA	21	189	110	5.3	.315	-2.0	LF(34): -6.3	-0.5
2019	HOU	MLB	22	62	91	0.4	.295	-0.1	1B 0	0.0

Seth Beer LF

Born: 09/18/96   Age: 22   Bats: L   Throws: R
Height: 6'3"   Weight: 195   Origin: Round 1, 2018 Draft (#28 overall)

YEAR	TEAM	LVL	AGE	PA	R	2B	3B	HR	RBI	BB	K	SB	CS	AVG/OBP/SLG
2018	TCV	A-	21	51	9	3	0	4	7	6	10	0	0	.293/.431/.659
2018	QUD	A	21	132	15	7	0	3	16	15	17	1	0	.348/.443/.491
2018	BCA	A+	21	114	15	4	0	5	19	4	22	0	1	.262/.307/.439
2019	HOU	MLB	22	251	27	7	0	9	26	10	62	0	0	.206/.247/.346

Breakout: 7%   Improve: 25%   Collapse: 1%   Attrition: 16%   MLB: 27%
Comparables: Austin Dean, Andrew Lambo, Anthony Santander

After his monstrous freshman season at Clemson in 2016, Beer seemed like he was the inevitable first pick in the 2018 Draft. He would never quite hit as well again in college. With a dab of indifferent defense and a dash of prospect fatigue mixed in, he ultimately fell to the latter stages of the first round. Despite this, he's quite a hitting prospect, with strong batting average and power projection and a discerning eye. His defense ... well, it might turn out to be fortunate that he was drafted by an American League club, if he can't settle into left field or first base. A minor concern to keep tabs on: Beer's vaunted plate discipline disappeared after his promotion to High-A. It's a smallish sample and many college players have tuckered out late in their draft year, so it's just a minor concern for now.

YEAR	TEAM	LVL	AGE	PA	DRC+	VORP	BABIP	BRR	FRAA	WARP
2018	TCV	A-	21	51	178	7.7	.296	-0.8	LF(7): -1.0, 1B(4): -0.1	0.1
2018	QUD	A	21	132	161	11.6	.391	-1.2	RF(10): -0.9, LF(9): -1.1	0.6
2018	BCA	A+	21	114	107	1.1	.288	-2.2	LF(13): -1.4, 1B(6): -0.2	-0.4
2019	HOU	MLB	22	251	59	-6.8	.241	-0.5	LF -1, 1B 0	-0.9

Freudis Nova SS

Born: 01/12/00   Age: 19   Bats: R   Throws: R
Height: 6'1"   Weight: 180   Origin: International Free Agent, 2016

YEAR	TEAM	LVL	AGE	PA	R	2B	3B	HR	RBI	BB	K	SB	CS	AVG/OBP/SLG
2017	DAR	ROK	17	190	30	6	0	4	16	15	33	8	3	.247/.342/.355
2018	AST	RK	18	157	21	3	1	6	28	6	21	9	5	.308/.331/.466
2019	HOU	MLB	19	251	23	4	0	7	21	1	67	3	1	.165/.172/.266

Breakout: 4%   Improve: 5%   Collapse: 0%   Attrition: 3%   MLB: 6%
Comparables: Gleyber Torres, Adalberto Mondesi, Wilmer Flores

Nova's story is a fine example of the sinking feeling you often get when looking too closely at international signings. For some time before the 2016-17 signing period opened, Nova was "connected" to the Marlins for a bonus around $2.5 million. If you've been following prospects for any length of time, you already know that's a euphemism for a deal agreed to well, well ahead of July 2, the legal time to sign the year's new crop 16-year-olds. Nova tested positive for performance-enhancing drugs before signing, and the Marlins cancelled the deal, leaving him adrift in the international pool with most of that cycle's money long-since locked up, and no recourse against the team that spurned him. The Astros, who were blowing well past their pool restrictions that year anyway, swooped in and signed Nova for $1.2 million. Two seasons and a lot of big reports out of the complex leagues later, Nova is emerging as a top prospect with offensive tools to spare and a good chance to stick somewhere on the dirt. Unless you're Juan Soto, the road from the Gulf Coast League to the majors is lengthy and has a lot of potholes, so the story might go many different ways from here.

YEAR	TEAM	LVL	AGE	PA	DRC+	VORP	BABIP	BRR	FRAA	WARP
2017	DAR	ROK	17	190	108	10.6	.287	-2.1		0.2
2018	AST	RK	18	157	126	9.8	.317	0.4	SS(24): -0.8, 2B(9): 0.0	0.4
2019	HOU	MLB	19	251	10	-18.3	.192	-0.2	SS -1, 2B 0	-2.0

A.J. Reed 1B

Born: 05/10/93 Age: 26 Bats: L Throws: L
Height: 6'4" Weight: 275 Origin: Round 2, 2014 Draft (#42 overall)

YEAR	TEAM	LVL	AGE	PA	R	2B	3B	HR	RBI	BB	K	SB	CS	AVG/OBP/SLG
2016	FRE	AAA	23	296	42	22	1	15	50	32	67	0	0	.291/.368/.556
2016	HOU	MLB	23	141	11	3	0	3	8	18	48	0	0	.164/.270/.262
2017	HOU	MLB	24	6	0	0	0	0	0	0	1	0	0	.000/.000/.000
2017	FRE	AAA	24	556	89	24	0	34	104	72	146	0	0	.261/.358/.525
2018	HOU	MLB	25	3	0	0	0	0	0	0	1	0	0	.000/.000/.000
2018	FRE	AAA	25	540	72	24	4	28	108	64	128	0	0	.255/.344/.506
2019	HOU	MLB	26	116	16	5	1	6	16	12	34	0	0	.235/.319/.480

Breakout: 2% Improve: 35% Collapse: 12% Attrition: 30% MLB: 65%
Comparables: Tyler Austin, Tommy Medica, Darin Ruf

The fall of a first base prospect can be swift and painful. Reed was our 55th-best prospect in baseball before the 2016 season, and likely would've ranked quite a bit higher on that year's midseason list were he not called up just before publication. To say that he was overmatched by major-league pitching would be putting it mildly. It's not like this sort of thing doesn't happen to good prospects in that small a sample—for example, Anthony Rizzo was just as bad in similar playing time as a rookie for the Padres in 2011. But Rizzo quickly got a change of scenery to a team that believed in him, whereas Reed's never gotten a clean opportunity for that second act, even when the Astros needed a power bat. He's dangerously close to falling into the Mike Hessman itinerant Quad-A slugger classification.

YEAR	TEAM	LVL	AGE	PA	DRC+	VORP	BABIP	BRR	FRAA	WARP
2016	FRE	AAA	23	296	135	20.1	.337	-2.4	1B(46): 2.2	0.9
2016	HOU	MLB	23	141	67	-7.2	.236	-0.2	1B(35): -2.0	-0.6
2017	HOU	MLB	24	6	78	-1.5	.000	0.0	1B(1): 0.0	0.0
2017	FRE	AAA	24	556	127	18.8	.299	-3.1	1B(109): -4.0	1.1
2018	HOU	MLB	25	3	85	-0.8	.000	0.0	1B(1): 0.0	0.0
2018	FRE	AAA	25	540	125	28.1	.285	-4.0	1B(90): -0.4	1.0
2019	HOU	MLB	26	116	101	2.1	.265	-0.2	1B -1	0.2

Houston Astros 2019

Myles Straw OF

Born: 10/17/94 Age: 24 Bats: R Throws: R
Height: 5'10" Weight: 180 Origin: Round 12, 2015 Draft (#349 overall)

YEAR	TEAM	LVL	AGE	PA	R	2B	3B	HR	RBI	BB	K	SB	CS	AVG/OBP/SLG
2016	QUD	A	21	307	40	14	6	0	22	29	58	17	10	.374/.432/.470
2016	LNC	A+	21	90	21	4	0	1	5	11	17	4	2	.303/.393/.395
2017	BCA	A+	22	533	81	17	7	1	41	87	70	36	9	.295/.412/.373
2017	CCH	AA	22	54	9	0	0	0	3	7	9	2	0	.239/.340/.239
2018	CCH	AA	23	294	47	7	3	1	17	35	42	35	6	.327/.414/.390
2018	FRE	AAA	23	304	48	10	3	0	14	38	60	35	3	.257/.349/.317
2018	HOU	MLB	23	10	4	0	0	1	1	1	0	2	0	.333/.400/.667
2019	HOU	MLB	24	30	4	1	0	0	2	3	7	2	0	.222/.300/.259

Breakout: 10%   Improve: 35%   Collapse: 1%   Attrition: 18%   MLB: 46%
Comparables: Boog Powell, Ezequiel Carrera, J.B. Shuck

At first blush, Straw may have seemed like an odd choice for a September call-up. Just 23, and with a well-known penchant for being a slap hitter, it would have been easy to question Houston's decision to see how Straw's game played in the bigs. But a little more scrolling would have revealed the truth: Myles Straw is very, very fast. It's true that stolen base totals are not a terrific measure of a player's speed, but Straw swiped 70 bags in 131 games between AA and AAA in 2018. (Whit Merrifield led the majors last year with 45. Modern baseball, man.) It's doubtful he will develop much power given his frame, but slap hitters are people, too. A young outfielder with defensive prowess and tons of speed will always have some value, especially when the rosters expand, and Straw has shown he has just that.

YEAR	TEAM	LVL	AGE	PA	DRC+	VORP	BABIP	BRR	FRAA	WARP
2016	QUD	A	21	307	170	29.1	.472	0.3	RF(24): 4.4, CF(21): 2.5	4.1
2016	LNC	A+	21	90	116	6.4	.373	2.7	RF(7): 1.1, CF(5): -0.6	0.6
2017	BCA	A+	22	533	149	54.3	.347	5.5	CF(72): 6.9, RF(31): 7.2	5.5
2017	CCH	AA	22	54	94	1.7	.297	0.6	CF(11): -1.1, LF(2): 0.7	0.0
2018	CCH	AA	23	294	141	24.6	.386	4.4	CF(58): 6.0, RF(6): 2.0	2.8
2018	FRE	AAA	23	304	94	8.1	.330	3.8	CF(43): 4.9, RF(25): 1.4	1.4
2018	HOU	MLB	23	10	108	1.9	.250	0.7	RF(5): -0.1, CF(3): 0.0	0.1
2019	HOU	MLB	24	30	57	0.0	.308	0.3	CF 0	0.0

Rogelio Armenteros   RHP

Born: 06/30/94   Age: 25   Bats: R   Throws: R
Height: 6'1"   Weight: 215   Origin: International Free Agent, 2014

YEAR	TEAM	LVL	AGE	W	L	SV	G	GS	IP	H	HR	BB/9	K/9	K	GB%	BABIP
2016	QUD	A	22	0	2	0	4	3	18^2	12	0	1.4	9.6	20	67%	.245
2016	LNC	A+	22	6	4	1	19	16	90^1	87	13	3.7	10.7	107	39%	.323
2016	CCH	AA	22	2	0	0	3	3	18^1	17	1	2.0	6.4	13	36%	.308
2017	CCH	AA	23	2	3	1	14	10	65^1	49	3	2.6	10.2	74	42%	.284
2017	FRE	AAA	23	8	1	0	10	10	58^1	42	5	2.9	11.1	72	50%	.276
2018	FRE	AAA	24	8	1	1	22	21	118	106	15	3.7	10.2	134	38%	.301
2019	HOU	MLB	25	3	2	0	21	6	46	40	6	3.7	9.7	50	39%	.287

Breakout: 10%   Improve: 29%   Collapse: 22%   Attrition: 25%   MLB: 62%
Comparables: Brian Johnson, Austin Voth, Nick Tropeano

Armenteros was not considered an elite Cuban prospect when the Astros took a $40,000 flier on him in 2014. Yet all he's done since is steadily march through the minors, racking up strikeouts, quality ERAs, and innings at every level. He's continued the trick in the upper levels, though his rates degraded a bit in the Pacific Coast League's tougher pitching environment. His spotty changeup has limited his ranking on prospect lists, but he's already shown durability, command of a useful fastball, and a big curveball. He's very close to being an MLB-quality pitcher right now, and how much his change improves will determine how high he can climb from there.

YEAR	TEAM	LVL	AGE	WHIP	ERA	DRA	WARP	MPH	FB%	WHF	CSP
2016	QUD	A	22	0.80	1.93	3.02	0.4				
2016	LNC	A+	22	1.37	4.18	5.06	0.4				
2016	CCH	AA	22	1.15	1.96	3.71	0.3				
2017	CCH	AA	23	1.04	1.93	2.93	1.7				
2017	FRE	AAA	23	1.05	2.16	1.97	2.4				
2018	FRE	AAA	24	1.31	3.74	3.59	2.6				
2019	HOU	MLB	25	1.25	4.01	4.39	0.5				

J.B. Bukauskas RHP
Born: 10/11/96 Age: 22 Bats: R Throws: R
Height: 6'0" Weight: 196 Origin: Round 1, 2017 Draft (#15 overall)

YEAR	TEAM	LVL	AGE	W	L	SV	G	GS	IP	H	HR	BB/9	K/9	K	GB%	BABIP
2017	TCV	A-	20	0	0	0	2	2	6	4	0	6.0	9.0	6	53%	.267
2018	TCV	A-	21	0	0	0	3	3	8^1	8	0	2.2	9.7	9	46%	.364
2018	QUD	A	21	1	2	0	4	4	15	15	0	4.2	12.6	21	55%	.395
2018	BCA	A+	21	3	0	0	5	5	28	13	1	4.2	10.0	31	59%	.194
2018	CCH	AA	21	0	0	0	1	1	6	1	0	3.0	12.0	8	60%	.100
2019	HOU	MLB	22	3	3	0	9	9	39^2	35	5	4.9	8.9	40	45%	.284

Breakout: 16% Improve: 23% Collapse: 5% Attrition: 16% MLB: 33%
Comparables: Carl Edwards Jr., Matt Moore, Trevor May

If this comment had been written right after the season, we might have made a joke about the dangers of saying his last name, and then segued into talk about another injury-plagued year for the flamethrower out of UNC. (This time, he missed half the season with an injured back from a car accident.) Instead, two far greater points of interest arose on Bukauskas as the leaves turned. First, he absolutely shoved in the Arizona Fall League, touching 98 mph with his fastball and reminding everyone that he still has one of the minors' best sliders. Then Ken Rosenthal of *The Athletic* reported that JBB was the proposed headliner in a deadline deal that would've sent Bryce Harper to the Astros, a trade that could've dramatically altered the American League playoffs. Both of those points hint at a buried lede: if Bukauskas can just stay healthy and throw strikes, he's one of the few pitchers in the minors with true top-of-the-rotation potential.

YEAR	TEAM	LVL	AGE	WHIP	ERA	DRA	WARP	MPH	FB%	WHF	CSP
2017	TCV	A-	20	1.33	4.50	3.27	0.1				
2018	TCV	A-	21	1.20	0.00	2.48	0.3				
2018	QUD	A	21	1.47	4.20	1.62	0.6				
2018	BCA	A+	21	0.93	1.61	3.13	0.7				
2018	CCH	AA	21	0.50	0.00	3.18	0.2				
2019	HOU	MLB	22	1.41	4.58	4.90	0.3				

Francis Martes   RHP

Born: 11/24/95   Age: 23   Bats: R   Throws: R
Height: 6'1"   Weight: 225   Origin: International Free Agent, 2012

YEAR	TEAM	LVL	AGE	W	L	SV	G	GS	IP	H	HR	BB/9	K/9	K	GB%	BABIP
2016	CCH	AA	20	9	6	0	25	22	125[1]	104	4	3.4	9.4	131	45%	.296
2017	FRE	AAA	21	0	2	0	8	8	32[1]	40	5	7.8	10.6	38	39%	.380
2017	HOU	MLB	21	5	2	0	32	4	54[1]	51	7	5.1	11.4	69	44%	.328
2018	FRE	AAA	22	0	1	0	4	4	18[2]	25	2	8.2	7.7	16	40%	.397
2019	HOU	MLB	23	2	2	0	11	6	33[2]	31	4	4.9	8.9	34	41%	.292

Breakout: 22%   Improve: 37%   Collapse: 16%   Attrition: 30%   MLB: 61%
Comparables: Randall Delgado, Marco Gonzales, Dana Eveland

Sometimes the path to Tommy John surgery goes quickly—a pitcher starts shaking his arm out on the mound, the MRI reveals a torn UCL, and surgery is scheduled for a week or two later. More often, it meanders on for some time. A pitcher will initially present with elbow discomfort, forearm tightness, or a flexor issue. The team will claim there is no structural damage, but he'll still be out for weeks or months. He'll come back for a little bit after rehabbing it and probably won't pitch all that well or reach his initial level. Then another MRI reveals the torn UCL. Martes started this cycle early on in the season when he reported elbow discomfort, and ended it in mid-August with Tommy John surgery, hitting the usual notes in between. He might pop up for a token appearance in 2019, but he's going to miss most or all of the season. Losing two seasons of development like this strikes a cruel blow to hopes that he might stick in the rotation.

YEAR	TEAM	LVL	AGE	WHIP	ERA	DRA	WARP	MPH	FB%	WHF	CSP
2016	CCH	AA	20	1.20	3.30	3.32	2.6				
2017	FRE	AAA	21	2.10	5.29	6.19	-0.2				
2017	HOU	MLB	21	1.51	5.80	4.39	0.6	97.8	55.4	13.5	46.7
2018	FRE	AAA	22	2.25	6.75	6.90	-0.3				
2019	HOU	MLB	23	1.46	4.68	5.01	0.2	97.7	57.4	14	48.3

Corbin Martin RHP

Born: 12/28/95 Age: 23 Bats: R Throws: R
Height: 6'2" Weight: 200 Origin: Round 2, 2017 Draft (#56 overall)

YEAR	TEAM	LVL	AGE	W	L	SV	G	GS	IP	H	HR	BB/9	K/9	K	GB%	BABIP
2017	TCV	A-	21	0	1	1	8	3	27^2	20	1	2.6	12.4	38	63%	.297
2018	BCA	A+	22	2	0	1	4	3	19	4	0	3.3	12.3	26	64%	.111
2018	CCH	AA	22	7	2	0	21	18	103	84	7	2.4	8.4	96	48%	.277
2019	HOU	MLB	23	3	2	0	8	8	40	37	5	3.5	8.7	39	47%	.290

Breakout: 17% Improve: 24% Collapse: 21% Attrition: 38% MLB: 58%
Comparables: Matt Magill, Giovanni Soto, Nestor Cortes

Martin's stock has been on a steady rise since he burst onto the prospect scene as a reliever in the Cape Cod League in the summer of 2016. He made a smooth transition into the rotation midway through the 2017 college season at Texas A&M, and the Astros rewarded him with a second-round draft selection and a cool million dollars in bonus money. He quickly sliced through A-ball like a hot knife through cold butter, and spent most of his first full pro campaign beating up on the Double-A Texas League. Despite a history that might tilt you towards projecting a future in the bullpen, the makings of a four-pitch mid-rotation starter are all already present here. We'll have to see if he can keep exceeding our projections.

YEAR	TEAM	LVL	AGE	WHIP	ERA	DRA	WARP	MPH	FB%	WHF	CSP
2017	TCV	A-	21	1.01	2.60	2.54	0.8				
2018	BCA	A+	22	0.58	0.00	3.10	0.5				
2018	CCH	AA	22	1.09	2.97	3.41	2.3				
2019	HOU	MLB	23	1.28	4.26	4.70	0.3				

Jairo Solis RHP

Born: 12/22/99   Age: 19   Bats: R   Throws: R
Height: 6'2"   Weight: 160   Origin: International Free Agent, 2016

YEAR	TEAM	LVL	AGE	W	L	SV	G	GS	IP	H	HR	BB/9	K/9	K	GB%	BABIP
2017	DAR	ROK	17	1	1	0	6	4	26^1	20	2	2.7	9.6	28	57%	.277
2017	AST	RK	17	1	0	0	5	4	21	19	1	3.0	10.3	24	43%	.305
2017	GRV	RK	17	1	1	0	4	2	14	12	0	3.9	10.9	17	36%	.333
2018	QUD	A	18	2	5	0	13	11	50^2	49	1	5.7	9.1	51	47%	.345
2019	HOU	MLB	19	2	3	0	16	8	42^2	43	7	6.4	7.9	37	42%	.293

Comparables: Kelvin Herrera, Alex Sanabia, Wilfredo Boscan

The projectable Venezuelan righty Solis spent his age-18 summer pitching in full-season ball, which is quite a bit more than you can say for most teenagers summering in Davenport, Iowa. And that's the allure of our heroic young arm: not what he is, but what he might be, what he might end up weighing and how hard he might end up throwing. At the moment, he has a fastball he can place and a curve that he doesn't necessarily have to, given the count. That's not enough to finish the story, but it's more than enough reason to keep turning pages.

YEAR	TEAM	LVL	AGE	WHIP	ERA	DRA	WARP	MPH	FB%	WHF	CSP
2017	DAR	ROK	17	1.06	2.73						
2017	AST	RK	17	1.24	3.00	3.88	0.5				
2017	GRV	RK	17	1.29	1.93	4.39	0.2				
2018	QUD	A	18	1.60	3.55	5.34	-0.1				
2019	HOU	MLB	19	1.73	6.19	6.67	-0.8				

Forrest Whitley RHP

Born: 09/15/97   Age: 21   Bats: R   Throws: R
Height: 6'7"   Weight: 195   Origin: Round 1, 2016 Draft (#17 overall)

YEAR	TEAM	LVL	AGE	W	L	SV	G	GS	IP	H	HR	BB/9	K/9	K	GB%	BABIP
2016	AST	RK	18	1	1	0	4	2	7[1]	8	0	3.7	16.0	13	29%	.471
2016	GRV	RK	18	0	1	0	4	4	11[1]	11	0	2.4	10.3	13	53%	.344
2017	QUD	A	19	2	3	0	12	10	46[1]	42	2	4.1	13.0	67	37%	.388
2017	BCA	A+	19	3	1	0	7	6	31[1]	28	2	2.6	14.4	50	40%	.394
2017	CCH	AA	19	0	0	0	4	2	14[2]	8	1	2.5	16.0	26	48%	.292
2018	CCH	AA	20	0	2	0	8	8	26[1]	15	2	3.8	11.6	34	39%	.220
2019	HOU	MLB	21	5	4	0	18	13	74	65	10	4.3	10.6	87	39%	.296

Breakout: 9%   Improve: 15%   Collapse: 8%   Attrition: 14%   MLB: 27%
Comparables: Jake McGee, Robert Stephenson, Trevor May

Baseball's top pitching prospect had the *Brooklyn Nine-Nine* of baseball seasons. Coming off a brilliant emergence, Whitley's first 50 games in 2018 were cancelled due to a drug suspension, and he later missed more time with oblique and lat problems. While it all combined to cost him his chance to make the majors before he could legally drink, the Arizona Fall League served as his NBC, a triumphant return just to remind everyone about all the plus pitches. He even touched triple digits in the Fall Stars game. He's only a handful of healthy and good starts away from The Show; exactly how many will depend on how aggressively his service time is manipulated. We can only hope *Nine-Nine*'s future is so bright.

YEAR	TEAM	LVL	AGE	WHIP	ERA	DRA	WARP	MPH	FB%	WHF	CSP
2016	AST	RK	18	1.50	7.36	1.53	0.3				
2016	GRV	RK	18	1.24	3.18	2.34	0.4				
2017	QUD	A	19	1.36	2.91	3.10	1.2				
2017	BCA	A+	19	1.18	3.16	2.06	1.2				
2017	CCH	AA	19	0.82	1.84	2.15	0.5				
2018	CCH	AA	20	0.99	3.76	3.49	0.6				
2019	HOU	MLB	21	1.36	4.18	4.60	0.7				

LINEOUTS

Hitters

HITTER	POS	TEAM	LVL	AGE	PA	R	2B	3B	HR	RBI	BB	K	SB	CS	AVG/OBP/SLG	DRC+	WARP
Ross Adolph	INF	BRO	A-	21	264	47	9	12	7	35	21	52	14	3	.276/.348/.509	146	1.4
Jose Alvarez	C	DAB	Rk	18	152	23	8	0	0	15	17	27	5	2	.359/.434/.420	165	1.2
Jonathan Arauz	SS	QUD	A	19	237	31	11	6	4	29	30	38	7	6	.299/.392/.471	147	1.9
	SS	BCA	A+	19	253	25	10	3	4	18	16	36	1	2	.167/.223/.288	39	-2.0
J.J. Matijevic	LF	QUD	A	22	56	8	6	1	3	5	8	10	3	0	.354/.446/.708	188	0.4
	LF	BCA	A+	22	376	58	20	3	19	57	36	103	10	13	.266/.335/.513	136	0.9
Alex McKenna	CF	TCV	A-	20	137	14	7	1	5	21	11	24	6	5	.328/.423/.534	178	1.0
	CF	QUD	A	20	51	5	1	1	2	7	3	16	0	0	.271/.314/.458	90	-0.2
Andy Pineda	LF	CCH	AA	21	71	9	2	1	2	6	4	16	3	3	.338/.394/.492	113	-0.1
	LF	TCV	A-	21	103	15	4	2	1	4	10	27	9	3	.253/.340/.374	109	0.2
Luis Santana	2B	KNG	Rk	18	242	34	13	0	4	35	27	23	8	3	.348/.446/.471	185	1.6
Garrett Stubbs	C	FRE	AAA	25	340	60	19	6	4	38	35	53	6	0	.310/.382/.455	117	3.2
Abraham Toro	3B	BCA	A+	21	349	54	20	1	14	56	45	62	5	1	.257/.361/.473	152	2.9
	3B	CCH	AA	21	202	16	15	2	2	22	17	46	3	3	.230/.317/.371	87	-0.5

Surprisingly athletic, leading the New York-Penn League in triples and isolated power—**Ross Adolph** wins both the award for best showing from the Mets' 2018 draft class and the Sterling Award for best player on the short-season Brooklyn Cyclones. ⓥ **Jose Alvarez** is a teenage catcher who hasn't been stateside yet, so in prospect terms, the light from him is so far away it hasn't reached earth. But what a fun batting line 2018 was! ⓥ Switch-hitting middle infielder **Jonathan Arauz** has a swing as graceful as the matador's cape, and carries about the same amount of weight behind it. ⓥ Astros 2017 second-rounder **J. J. Matijevic** swings a lot, shows a good deal of power, and offers the defensive value of someone who swings a lot and shows a good deal of power. Imagine if C.J. Cron were younger and had a name that was much harder to spell. ⓥ Big West Conference Player of the Year **Alex McKenna** raked nearly as much with wooden bats in his pro debut as he did with the composite bats at Cal Poly. ⓥ Houston drafted **Joe Perez** in 2017's second round knowing he'd need Tommy John surgery. He's only made a cameo appearance in the GCL to date, and the toolsy prepster could yet end up on the mound instead of in the infield. ⓥ **Andy Pineda** doesn't look like a power hitter (5 career home runs in a thousand plate appearances), but his outs go farther than you'd expect, and that combined with the hit tool marks him as perhaps the deepest sleeper in this book. ⓥ So far, the only thing that 19-year-old **Luis Santana** has done consistently is make contact in the low minors. That's no small feat, but his bat-to-ball ability will have to carry him a long way, as his short stature and limited physical gifts make him a second-base-only prospect without other carrying tools. ⓥ **Garrett Stubbs** is well-positioned to join the fraternity of long-term backup catchers,

Houston Astros 2019

though he possesses sneaky athleticism and a sprinkle of hitting potential to go along with the pre-installed nickname and the usual strong defensive reputation. Ⓥ **Abraham Toro** Trilingual Montreal native was drafted out of Seminole State College in Oklahoma, the same school as fellow Quebecer Eric Gagne. May he match Gagne's utter brilliance in the majors some day.

Pitchers

PITCHER	TEAM	LVL	AGE	W	L	SV	G	GS	IP	H	HR	BB/9	K/9	K	GB%	WHIP	ERA	DRA	WARP
Brett Adcock	BCA	A+	22	5	3	1	16	9	67^1	32	1	4.8	9.0	67	49%	1.01	2.54	3.21	1.6
	CCH	AA	22	4	2	0	9	5	38^2	34	2	5.1	6.5	28	35%	1.45	3.49	4.44	0.3
Brandon Bielak	BCA	A+	22	5	3	2	14	7	55^2	44	2	2.7	12.0	74	43%	1.10	2.10	2.50	1.7
	CCH	AA	22	2	5	0	11	10	61^1	52	4	3.2	8.4	57	51%	1.21	2.35	4.18	0.8
Dean Deetz	FRE	AAA	24	2	0	0	21	0	34	22	1	4.8	13.2	50	49%	1.18	0.79	2.52	1.0
	HOU	MLB	24	0	0	0	4	0	3^1	4	1	2.7	8.1	3	30%	1.50	5.40	6.63	-0.1
Reymin Guduan	FRE	AAA	26	3	3	2	43	0	55^1	46	5	5.2	13.5	83	55%	1.41	3.74	1.82	2.1
	HOU	MLB	26	0	0	0	3	0	3^1	1	1	0.0	10.8	4	14%	0.30	2.70	2.91	0.1
Ryan Hartman	CCH	AA	24	11	4	0	25	18	120^2	104	11	1.9	10.7	143	43%	1.08	2.69	2.76	3.5
Tyler Ivey	QUD	A	22	1	3	2	9	6	41^2	36	2	1.7	11.4	53	50%	1.06	3.46	2.29	1.4
	BCA	A+	22	3	3	1	15	12	70^1	50	3	2.7	10.5	82	56%	1.01	2.69	2.92	1.9
Ernesto Jaquez	DAB	Rk	19	4	0	0	9	4	36	10	0	2.2	12.2	49	63%	0.53	0.25	1.33	1.7
	AST	Rk	19	0	0	0	5	1	17	9	1	2.6	11.1	21	46%	0.82	1.06	2.65	0.6
Cristian Javier	QUD	A	21	2	2	1	11	7	49^1	28	3	4.2	14.6	80	32%	1.03	1.82	2.00	1.8
	BCA	A+	21	5	4	0	14	11	60^2	44	6	4.0	9.8	66	33%	1.17	3.41	3.28	1.4
Brady Rodgers	BCA	A+	27	0	0	0	4	4	12	12	0	0.0	5.2	7	59%	1.00	1.50	2.55	0.4
	FRE	AAA	27	3	3	0	8	8	41	48	4	2.2	6.6	30	38%	1.41	5.49	4.43	0.5
Jayson Schroeder	AST	Rk	18	0	0	0	7	5	18	13	0	4.5	9.0	18	49%	1.22	1.50	4.02	0.4

Brett Adcock has battled walks since he was a Michigan Man, but as a lefty with a good curve he'll get enough shots to need to Uber it home from the bar. Ⓥ **Brandon Bielak** has better stuff than the usual late-round college pitcher shooting through the minors, and has a chance to contribute soon, likely in a relief role. Ⓥ **Dean Deetz** returned from an 80-game PED suspension as a dominant Triple-A reliever, eventually making the majors in September. In so doing he fulfilled years of Wilson Karaman's predictions that he'd eventually figure out how to harness his big fastball and wipeout breaking ball. Ⓥ It's hard to imagine the Astros actually needing **Reymin Guduan**, but he's here, he's left-handed and he throws hard. Some other team will eventually give him a chance to figure out the strike zone in some 8-3 losses. Ⓥ **Ryan Hartman** doesn't impress the scouts with his stuff, but that production at Double-A is just over the line of "let's wait and see how long it takes him to start failing." ⚾ **Tyler Ivey** has four pitches, throws strikes, and breezed through A-ball, but he'll need to pass that age-old Double-A test before we go all in. ⚾ **Ernesto Jaquez's** (very) brief taste of A-ball was a bit too spicy, but the teenager's prior performance and ability to command four pitches make his name one worth filing away. ⚾ These days on the minors beat you'll see a ton of young pitchers who clearly grew up watching either Pedro Martinez or Cole Hamels, and well, **Cristian Javier** is a Dominican righty with a change and a very familiar looking motion. He even wore number 45 for Quad Cities. ⚾ **Brady Rodgers** had just barely reached the top of the ladder when he was felled by a second TJS in 2017. He looked as good as ever in his late-2018 rehab, which is to say, he looked like a command-oriented, pitch-to-contact seventh starter. ⚾ If you've made it this far in, you can probably guess that the future for second-rounder **Jayson Schroeder** is pretty bright given Houston's wildly successful recent track record with identifying and developing projectable arms.

Astros Prospects

The State of the System:
The Astros system is on the rise again due to improvements across the board from their deep well of pitching prospects.

The Top Ten:

1 **Forrest Whitley   RHP**   OFP: 70   Likely: 60
ETA: Should be on the opening day squad for 2019.
Born: 09/15/97   Age: 21   Bats: R   Throws: R   Height: 6'7"   Weight: 195
Origin: Round 1, 2016 Draft (#17 overall)

The Report: How many times do we need to say that Forrest Whitley is good? I guess one more time before he dons an Astros jersey and never looks back won't hurt.

Whitley is a plus athlete with excellent quick twitch, body control, and strength. The days where his body was described as soft are gone, and he's now impressively filled out with a towering frame on the mound.

The right-hander works 94-97 with the fastball with some arm-side life on it. It can be hard to pick up, as Whitley comes from over the top and releases out in front with good extension. Whitley has two distinct plus breaking balls, one at 80-81 with traditional curveball spin and break, one 85-87 with sharp dive. Whitley throws a plus changeup with deceptive arm speed and plus tumble and fade. He occasionally mixes in a 91-93 above-average cutter that he likes to break off the plate against righties to get whiffs later after they've gotten a few looks at his regular fastball.

If there's one place to look for weakness in the profile, it's the command. Whitley has pretty consistent feel for all of his offerings, but he can struggle to locate at any given time. His fastball location in particular is spotty and he's prone to falling behind early in counts.

Overall though, Whitley is the best pitching prospect in baseball. He has five above-average or better offerings, giving him a tremendous ceiling and high floor despite the command concerns. He's one of the few pitchers in the sport with elite upside, and he can get there if his command ticks up a grade.

The Risks: Low. The arsenal is so deep, it's just hard to see him not being an effective MLB starter even with some command issues. Pitches in an org that will let him pitch backwards if he needs to lean away from fastball.

Ben Carsley's Fantasy Take: Thanks to his strikeout upside and proximity to the majors, we ranked Whitley as the best pitching prospect in baseball on our Dynasty Top 101 list. That doesn't necessarily mean he'll reach true fantasy SP1 status, but we think he has a chance to do so in his peak years. Be happy to "settle" for more of a fantasy SP2/3 performance in the mold of what Mike Foltynewicz did last season, and treat anything else as the gravy on top. He's great.

2. Kyle Tucker   OF

OFP: 70   Likely: 60   ETA: Debuted in 2018
Born: 01/17/97   Age: 22   Bats: L   Throws: R   Height: 6'4"   Weight: 190
Origin: Round 1, 2015 Draft (#5 overall)

The Report: Kyle Tucker's profile doesn't jump off the board at first glance. His 6'4" frame looks more lanky than lean, he has a laid back demeanor, and he lacks flashy foot speed.

But Tucker gets the barrel on the ball as well as anyone. His quickness, plus bat speed, and barrel control allow him to make consistently hard contact. He has plus raw power and he's made the kind of adjustments in his swing that suggest he'll get to all of it in games. Tucker's pitch recognition is subpar, but he made tremendous strides last year to both improve his selectiveness and recognize spin. Overall, Tucker projects as a 70 bat. Between that, improving walk rates, and his raw power, he could develop into an offensive force.

His defense in the corner outfield is considerably less exciting. He has below-average speed, and despite decent instincts, that translates into below-average range. He makes good reads, takes efficient routes, and has a strong arm, so he isn't a complete disaster in a corner. He should be average or just a bit worse in right or left. Regardless, Tucker's work at the plate will get him in the lineup. If his plate discipline takes a step forward, he could be a perennial all-star.

The Risks: Low: Unlike many who have concerns about the profile after a sluggish start, I've seen Tucker make adjustments over a season or two. I'm not concerned about him, and expect him to settle into a big-league lineup as soon as he gets a consistent opportunity.

Ben Carsley's Fantasy Take: We ranked Tucker as a top-10 overall dynasty prospect on the strength of his hit tool, speed, power and proximity to the majors. He is perhaps the safest bet of anyone in the minors to at least become a fantasy OF3, and there's borderline fantasy OF1 upside here for those seasons in which it all clicks. Although they're quite different physically, Tucker comps fairly well to Andrew Benintendi from a fantasy POV, with an even higher ceiling. He should be a mainstay for our purposes by June.

3. Josh James   RHP
OFP: 60   Likely: 50   ETA: Debuted in 2018
Born: 03/08/93   Age: 26   Bats: R   Throws: R   Height: 6'3"   Weight: 206
Origin: Round 34, 2014 Draft (#1006 overall)

The Report: Here's the most improbable prospect rise of 2018. After getting treatment for sleep apnea and improving his health, James spiked his stuff by about 10 MPH and in the process went from an organizational player to a mid-tier 101 prospect. Now we just have to figure out where he settles in.

James now throws a 96-98 mph fastball with some arm-side life, especially when working that side of the plate, and he touched 101 in the majors in September. His best secondary is a hard slider at 85-87 mph. It flashes plus with plus horizontal break and spin, and with a little depth too. His 87-89 mph changeup also flashes plus. At present, James has below-average command and it's hard to project definite improvement there, given his high-maintenance delivery.

The raw stuff and velocity from James is strong enough to overcome the command issues he will likely carry into his MLB career. A high-90's fastball and two pitches that project as plus secondaries suggest a future in the rotation, but even if he isn't a starter, he should transition well into a high-leverage relief role.

The Risks: Low, since he's already an MLB arm. Even if his command plays down more than I expect in the starting rotation, he has an excellent bullpen repertoire and should seamlessly shift into that role.

Ben Carsley's Fantasy Take: One of the more intriguing pop-up prospects from 2018, James is ready to contribute now, and indeed looks like he should compete for a spot in Houston's starting rotation. If he wins one, he could emerge as an excellent all-around fantasy SP3 in the Mike Clevinger mold. If not, James has closer upside but is perhaps more likely to settle in as a setup man, which would give us a serious sadz. Let's hope Houston gives him every chance to succeed as a starter.

4. Yordan Alvarez   1B
OFP: 60   Likely: 50   ETA: September 2019
Born: 06/27/97   Age: 22   Bats: L   Throws: R   Height: 6'5"   Weight: 225
Origin: International Free Agent, 2016

The Report: Alvarez is long and strong with more athleticism than meets the eye. He posts surprisingly solid home-to first-times, and he's twitchy with impressive body control. Even if he adds a couple more pounds in the next few years, they might come without a corresponding reduction in mobility.

Alvarez has plus barrel control and bat speed, which allows him to mostly compensate for a long swing. He still can get beat on velocity inside and up if he's caught off guard, but he tends to fight the pitch off pretty well most of the time. He's patient and isn't afraid to let close pitches go by; if anything, a bit more aggressiveness would be appropriate. He struggles somewhat with breaking stuff and offspeed, but showed an aptitude for making adjustments both over a season and in games. Alvarez doesn't tap fully into his double-plus raw power, as a great deal of his hardest contact comes on line drives, but he should provide plus power regardless.

Alvarez has the hands and reactions to be an above-average first baseman and the foot speed to be fringy in a corner outfield spot. First is his long-term home though, and Alvarez's bat and approach should allow him to provide above-average value there.

The Risks: Medium. Yordan has good offensive tools, makes adjustments, and has a good approach. The main concern is how much MLB pitchers will be able to take advantage of the small holes in the swing.

Ben Carsley's Fantasy Take: Alvarez is a good fantasy prospect—we ranked him at no. 25 overall in our Top 101—but that's largely because we think he's safe and will be ready to hit soon. I don't see any star upside with Alvarez, but I do think he could be a more athletic 2017 Josh Bell-like player who hits .275 with 25-plus bombs, and who hopefully retains dual 1B/OF eligibility throughout his early career. That may not sound super exciting, but let a player with those underlying skills hit in Houston's lineup and at Minute Maid and you've got the makings of a four-category fantasy force.

5. J.B. Bukauskas   RHP

OFP: 60   Likely: 50   ETA: Late 2019
Born: 10/11/96   Age: 22   Bats: R   Throws: R   Height: 6'0"   Weight: 196
Origin: Round 1, 2017 Draft (#15 overall)

The Report: The party piece here is a plus-plus slider, one of the best non-fastball pitches in the entire minors. It falls off the table in a way that is difficult for hitters to read, and it comes in hard at 86-88. He pairs that with a diving fastball that sat 95-98 in the Arizona Fall League, and a hard, cutting changeup that is more than just a show-me type pitch. It's a strong pitch mix, and more than good enough for rotation work.

Despite that, the major question here is whether JBB can start. He missed most of the 2018 regular season due to back injuries suffered in a spring car accident, and he wasn't really right until the end of the year and in the AFL. Bukauskas is short and doesn't generate a lot of plane, and his delivery has enough jerky violence to make one pause on visual inspection. He might just fit best blowing folks away with the fastball and slider for 20 pitches or so.

As a creative team open to amorphous pitching roles, Houston is well-positioned to find a role in which he can thrive and stay healthy—if they keep him. We learned after the season from The Athletic's Ken Rosenthal that Houston nearly traded JBB at the deadline to borrow Bryce Harper's services for the stretch, a deal nixed by ownership in Washington.

The Risks: Medium because of health and difficulty in projecting a role. On skill the floor is high, because we think he could pitch well in an MLB bullpen tomorrow.

Ben Carsley's Fantasy Take: If you think Bukauskas can start, he's a top-60ish dynasty prospect who you will likely prefer over safer guys with less upside like Kyle Wright, Adrian Morejon and Chris Paddack. Unfortunately, I believe Bukauskas' future lies in the bullpen, which is why I did not push to rank him on our list. I'd love to be proven wrong, because this is a live, fun arm, and one definitely still worth gambling on if you roster 150-or-so prospects in your league.

6. Corbin Martin   RHP
OFP: 55   Likely: 50   ETA: September 2019
Born: 12/28/95   Age: 23   Bats: R   Throws: R   Height: 6'2"   Weight: 200
Origin: Round 2, 2017 Draft (#56 overall)

The Report: Martin fits the mould of a mid-rotation arm to a tee. He has an athletic build with a high waist and strong core. He's a quality athlete, and throws three strong, if not overpowering, pitches from a clean arm and delivery.

Martin sits 91-94 with his four-seamer. Most of the time, he has average command of his fastball and mixes in the other two offerings off of it, but sometimes he'll pitch backwards and use it high in the zone later in counts. Martin mixes in an almost vertical 83-85 slider with plus dive and a changeup that flashes above-average with deceptive arm speed and some tumble and fade.

Pitchibility is Martin's bread and butter. He's comfortable mixing speeds, using the same tunnel for the slider and changeup, and throwing first-pitch strikes with his fastball or slider. When he loses his release point, he's comfortable pitching backwards and turning to his secondaries. All three pitches are above-average or better. He projects as a quality No. 4 starter, perhaps a tick more if he refines his command.

The Risks: Low. Already has the pitch mix and showed much improved command in 2018.

Ben Carsley's Fantasy Take: Martin has proximity on his side, but upside… not so much. He is adrift amidst the sea of IRL no. 4 and fantasy no. 6/7 starters who'd probably occupy about 40 percent of a theoretical Top 101-through-201 list. At least we should have a pretty good idea as to who he is and what he can do sooner rather than later.

7. Freudis Nova   SS
OFP: 60   Likely: 45   ETA: 2023
Born: 01/12/00   Age: 19   Bats: R   Throws: R   Height: 6'1"   Weight: 180
Origin: International Free Agent, 2016

The Report: If Nova's namesake was a prospect writer he might have instead written: "Complex-league shortstops have no obvious use; nor is there any clear cultural necessity for them. Yet prospect lists could not do without them." Nova fell into the Astros lap after a reported failed drug test scuttled his deal with the Marlins, and he's been a steady performer as a pro so far. The horizon to major-league contribution is long here, and he's not super likely to be a big breakout guy. While he has good tools, they're more moderately loud, average-to-above across the board. He already shows plus bat speed and loud contact and there's plenty of reason to believe he will grow into above-average power as he matures. Nova is another for the "maybe" bucket at shortstop and he's already gotten reps at second and third as a pro. The bat may be good enough to carry any of the infield spots, but it's human nature to try and overfit narrative stories to even the fuzziest of dreams.

The Risks: Extreme. Complex league resume only here.

Ben Carsley's Fantasy Take: Nova remains an intriguing prospect who had a strong 2018 season in the GCL. He's yet to be truly challenged, but could be a sneaky top-101 candidate next season if he repeats his performance against more advanced arms. Guys like this tend to get forgotten in favor of the shinier/newer J2 and draft classes; they shouldn't be.

8. Seth Beer   1B

OFP: 55   Likely: 50   ETA: 2020
Born: 09/18/96   Age: 22   Bats: L   Throws: R   Height: 6'3"   Weight: 195
Origin: Round 1, 2018 Draft (#28 overall)

The Report: Beer was the most ballyhooed freshman ballplayer in recent memory after his .369/.535/.700 performance in 2016 for Clemson. He was still a fine, fine player for the Tigers after that, but he never quite lived up to the first impression, and ultimately fell quite a bit from the early predictions that had him going 1.1 in 2018.

If you liked watching various members of the Giambi family play the big-league version of beer-league softball (pun intended) back in the day, this is your dude. Beer combines rare patience for his age with plus-plus power that he brings into games. There's some disagreement over the hit tool projection. If you like him, you can point to a smooth swing with good bat speed. If you don't, you can point to more swing-and-miss than you'd like given the rest of the offensive profile. For the time being, we're going to split the difference and acknowledge the validity in both arguments. He's probably going to hit a lot.

We have Beer listed as primarily a first baseman here, even though he played more left than first after signing. He's not an outfielder in any real sense, and he might not even be a first baseman. The Astros play in the DH league, and we do think he's going to hit, but don't be surprised if the positional appellation switches to designated hitter pretty soon. It might even be before he graduates.

The Risks: Low. There's profile risk in that the bat is going to really have to carry the mail here, but this is about as low risk of a hitting profile as you can get out of the draft. He should move quickly—through the system, that is; he's not much of a runner.

Ben Carsley's Fantasy Take: I really hope he reaches his full potential for the fantasy team name pun potential alone. Realistically it's tough for these DH-types to matter much—that's a lesson I'm trying very hard to take away from The Dan Vogelbach Experience. But if Beer does end up hitting nearly every day, he could bash 35-plus bombs with a fine average. That'd make him rosterable in any league format, but just beware that that's his ceiling, and there's a very low platoon/bench bat floor here too.

9 Cionel Perez   LHP

OFP: 50   Likely: 45   ETA: Debuted in 2018
Born: 04/21/96   Age: 23   Bats: L   Throws: L   Height: 5'11"   Weight: 170
Origin: International Free Agent, 2016

The Report: Cionel Perez is a small guy with a lanky build, and he still hasn't really filled out. Despite that, he's a solid athlete who can control a fairly noisy delivery and arm action from the left side better than you'd expect.

Perez sits around 94 with the fastball that comes from a tricky slot on the left side. He likes to work toward the arm-side of the plate and tends to have better command of the pitch there as well. He doesn't miss the zone much, but when he tries to go in on righties he leaves the pitch over the plate fairly often.

Perez mixes in two breaking balls, an above-average 83-84 slider with two-plane movement and a fringy 12-6 curveball in the upper-70s that floats when left up in the zone. He throws a fringe-average changeup that has some fade, but hitters can usually recognize it well enough to fight it off even when he locates well.

Perez's control is well ahead of his command at this point: he doesn't struggle to throw strikes, but he's not terribly precise. His delivery is loud enough that it's hard to see it improving down the road and it will likely keep him out of a starting rotation long term.

Perez has the tools and the repertoire to be an effective one-time-through-the-order or low-setup pitcher in an MLB bullpen. The fastball-slider combo will be tough on lefties, but he doesn't have a lot to neutralize righties with. Ultimately, there are a lot of productive directions his career can go, even if most of them are in a relief role of some sort.

The Risks: Medium. The command and curveball consistency leaves two important pieces to be cleaned up before breaking into the big leagues. His fastball isn't overpowering enough to leave as much middle/middle as he does, especially given the lack of secondaries to compensate with against righties.

Ben Carsley's Fantasy Take: Get this Present Day Martin Perez-ass dynasty prospect out of my face, please.

10 Framber Valdez   LHP

OFP: 50   Likely: 45   ETA: Debuted in 2018
Born: 11/19/93   Age: 25   Bats: L   Throws: L   Height: 5'11"   Weight: 170
Origin: International Free Agent, 2015

The Report: Our reports and rankings exist in a vacuum. So we don't consider that Brendan Rodgers will be playing his home game in Coors or that DL Hall is in a system that hasn't developed a starting pitching prospect since Mike

Mussina. The only context is the prospect and what they can do. That said, Framber Valdez is in the right organization to get the most out of spamming an advanced curveball, as is his wont.

It's a potential plus curveball as well. While not the biggest breaker, the 1-7 action is tight and late and Valdez commands it well. He's not a soft tosser either, touching 95 from the left side with some sink when he's down in the zone. The delivery is a bit on the stiff side, the frame is a bit on the thick side, and his age is a bit on the old side. And we do need to consider this context: As an Astros pitching prospect he tends to see shorter outings, so even if there weren't already some bullpen markers here, we'd have no idea if he can hold up under a full starter's workload. Houston does seem to get a lot out of this general profile though [gestures wildly up and down the rest of this list], and it is a very nice curveball.

The Risks: Low. Valdez pitched well in the upper minors and while there's significant relief risk, the fastball/curve combo is just about ready for the Houston metroplex.

Ben Carsley's Fantasy Take: How many times do I need to tell you not to invest in back-end starter prospects?

The Next Five:

11
Rogelio Armenteros   RHP
Born: 06/30/94   Age: 25   Bats: R   Throws: R   Height: 6'1"   Weight: 215
Origin: International Free Agent, 2014

Rogelio takes a bit of a tumble down the list, but that's more due to the system strengthening around him than any potholes along his development path. It's also probably for the best that Jarrett had lead on this list as I'd perhaps be inclined to over-rank Armenteros due to the #aesthetics here, which are extremely Yusmeiro Petitish. As I like to say, "it's not a pref list, except when it's a pref list." Rogelio is a hefty righty as well with an easy delivery, averageish fastball and breaker, and a potential plus change. Frankly, that's more prospect-Petit than major-leaguer-Petit, but that only helps with the aesthetics. He hits the glove without issue and misses more bats than you'd think, but the profile is always going to have fine margins as a FB/CH righty with only an average heater. Yusmeiro Petit's career is maybe more like a 40th percentile outcome here, as we still think Rogelio has a chance to be a back-end starter. But hey, that below-median outcome came with eight-figure income and a World Series ring last time.

12
Luis Santana   2B
Born: 07/20/99   Age: 19   Bats: R   Throws: R   Height: 5'8"   Weight: 175
Origin: International Free Agent, 2016

Santana is the first of two prospects on this list acquired recently from the Mets in the J.D. Davis trade. He will go as far as his hit tool takes him, and in that way, Santana is reminiscent of another R/R second baseman from his former organization, T.J. Rivera. Rivera—an undrafted free agent who was significantly overage at every minor league stop—has almost nothing else in common with Santana, but the former's unlikely path to the majors offers a roadmap for the latter. Let's cover the issues with the profile first. Santana is not 5-foot-8 for starters; he's more likely a stocky 5-foot-6. He's a fringy runner with below-average power. He's good enough at second base, but his arm strength is below-average and his throws can get casual.

He also hit .350 in the Appy League and didn't turn 19 until a month into the season. He barrels everything he sees. At a glance, it sure looks like a potential plus hit tool. But Santana's swing is… noisy. His hands are in constant motion pre-swing, and while he ends up short to the ball, I wonder how that bat path will work as he sees more dudes throwing 95. It's a very tough profile, but a plus hit tool will paper over a lot of faults. And for Santana it might be enough to make him an average regular in the majors.

13 Ross Adolph   OF
Born: 12/17/96   Age: 22   Bats: L   Throws: R   Height: 6'1"   Weight: 203
Origin: Round 12, 2018 Draft (#350 overall)

The second player acquired for Davis lies just below him on this list, just as he did on the Mets list. The Mets popped Adolph—a first team All-MAC player—in the 12th round in 2018 and gave him full pool. I was prepared to be unimpressed; however, he won me over almost immediately, showing average tools across the board. Despite a stocky physique, he's an above-average runner with a high motor who can go get it in center field. He's short to the ball with sneaky pop that plays pull side and oppo gap. He stays in well against lefties. There's no plus tool here, and the profile screams 'tweener,' but Adolph projects as a quality fourth outfielder who might surprise you (and me) and end up a second-division type.

14 Jonathan Arauz   SS
Born: 08/03/98   Age: 20   Bats: B   Throws: R   Height: 6'0"   Weight: 150
Origin: International Free Agent, 2014

It was a tale of two seasons for Arauz. In the first half, the 19-year-old was one of the better players in the Midwest League. In the second, sandwiched around his 20th birthday, he was one of the worst players in the Carolina League. It was an aggressive promotion, and he's too good to give up on. We were concerned about his propensity to make weak contact last year, and that certainly actualized some, but a .180 BABIP in High-A is ridiculous even by that standard. Arauz has already been exposed to second and third, and carries with him a decent bundle of secondary hitting skills, but he's going to have to start driving the ball with more authority to beat the "utility dude" projection.

15 **Abraham Toro 3B**
Born: 12/20/96 Age: 22 Bats: B Throws: R Height: 6'1" Weight: 190
Origin: Round 5, 2016 Draft (#157 overall)

Two decades ago, a Montreal-area native by way of Seminole State College in Oklahoma exploded on the prospect scene. Eric Gagne would go on to become one of baseball's rare Cy Young closers, a monster of a reliever until he got hurt. Toro followed the same path, from a Montreal high school to Seminole State to the Astros. He's not quite on Gagne's level as a prospect and stands little chance to get there, but he's a nifty player in his own right.

The former fifth-rounder combines average pop with a good feel for the bat. He has a solid understanding of the strike zone, and played well in last year's AFL. He should stick at third base, and he even dabbled a little with catching in 2017, enough that he should be fine to handle a third catcher role in the majors. He's not likely to be a star, and cracking the Astros lineup with this skill set isn't going to be easy, but he has a shot to be someone's regular third baseman for awhile.

Others of note:

Alex McKenna, OF Short-season Tri-City

The Astros popped McKenna in 2018's fourth round and, oddly for a college junior in that part of the draft, he got slightly over slot value to sign. McKenna was a star hitter at Cal Poly for most of his college career, winning the Big West Player of the Year award in 2018, and he also performed well in 2017 with wood bats on the Cape. He's a solid all-around hitter with some athleticism, versatility between the outfield slots, and sneaky power. More interestingly, he looked to be adding some loft to his swing as a pro. There's a lot of similarity here between McKenna and Adolph, both college-performer outfielders who torched the New York-Penn League in their pro debuts. The Astros do have a type.

Jairo Solis, RHP Low-A Quad Cities

The Astros tend to exercise more caution with their pitchers than most teams, and they've done very well with pitcher development in general. In that vein, Solis was one of the most lightly used "starters" in the minors. He was held back in extended until late-May, frequently went on extra rest, and never once pierced 100 pitches or went past the sixth inning. All that care... and it didn't matter anyway, as he went down with Tommy John surgery after being shut down in August. He'll miss the entire 2019 season. Before the surgery, Solis was a low-to-mid-90s righty with a potentially plus curve and average or better change. He did pitch decently as an 18-year-old in full-season ball, so he won't be far behind developmentally when he returns in 2020; it still stinks.

Top Talents 25 and Under (born 4/1/93 or later):

1. Carlos Correa
2. Forrest Whitley
3. Kyle Tucker
4. Josh James
5. Roberto Osuna
6. Yordan Alvarez
7. Francis Martes
8. J.B. Bukauskas
9. Corbin Martin
10. Freudis Nova

Don't worry about the Astros. Sure, the first homegrown rebuild crop doesn't quite have the green shoots of youth anymore: George Springer turns 30 this year, Altuve will be 29, and of course the 34-year-old Yuli Gurriel came over with plenty of Cuban League wear-and-tear. But the Astros will keep the line moving, as Whitley, Tucker, and James are set to add a timely infusion of fresh arms and bats.

March 30th birthday boy Alex Bregman misses this list by roughly 48 hours, otherwise he might—given last season's growth—have nosed out Correa for top honors here. As it is, Correa is the clear headliner, injury worries aside. 2019 will be a pivotal season for the former first-overall pick. If healthy, he'll be expected to pick up his interrupted trajectory toward superstardom, forming an infield left-side whose only competition for supremacy would be the Ramirez-Lindor pairing in Cleveland. The fact that Correa is still on this list, even with more than 2,000 major-league plate appearances under his belt, prompts a degree of optimism for his full recovery. We won't dwell on darker, Tulowitzkian timelines in this space.

Osuna comes in halfway through this list. He is still a hard-throwing closer with a devastating slider, but closers are commodities with a limited shelf life and a sharp decrease in his strikeout rate bears watching. In an unjust irony, his 75-game suspension for a domestic assault incident in May gave some rest to an arm that had been used for nearly 260 high-leverage innings over the previous three years.

Francis Martes, BP's #28 prospect heading into 2017, spent significant time that summer in the Astros bullpen, striking out plenty but walking far too many. Soon after the 2018 season began, a rough start in Triple-A spiraled into a blown UCL and Tommy John surgery. He probably won't pitch much in 2019, but the promise of future health, plus the recent memory of the lights-out prospect he was before his elbow revolted, puts him in a holding pattern on this list for the time being.

Folks, the Astros are still great. Folding the prospects near the top of this list into the current late-twenties core will keep them at short odds for championship hardware well into the next decade—assuming there's still baseball to care about then.

Part 3: Featured Articles

The Hole in The Shift is Fixing Itself

Russell Carleton

I've been on a bit of a mission against The Shift of late. I'm not out to get The Shift for the usual reasons that people oppose it. The words "the right way to play the game" won't be found on my lips. If a team wants to pursue a strategy that is within the rules and it works, then by all means, they have my blessing (not that they need it). Instead, my concern with The Shift is a worry that it doesn't work, or at least that it has a flaw that needs fixing.

The data show that while The Shift does a decent job of preventing singles on balls in play (what it's supposed to do), it also increases the number of walks that happen in front of it, and the number of additional walks outweighs the number of singles saved. It's a problem because you can't throw a guy out if he gets to walk to first base.

But the "why" was important. It seemed that The Shift was changing the way in which pitchers pitched. We saw that there were fewer fastballs thrown in front of The Shift than we might otherwise expect, and that pitchers tended to stay out of the strike zone a little more. Not by a lot. In fact, it might not even be visible to the naked eye. The percentage of pitches that are out of the zone goes from 51.0 to 53.3 from a standard defense (two right/two left) to a full shift (three on one side). That difference stands up even after we control for the types of hitters that get shifted against. And it's enough to drive up the walk rate to where it cancels out the benefits that teams thought they were getting with The Shift... and then some.

But there was some hope. I found that when individual pitchers stayed closer to the in-zone/out-of-zone mix that they used without The Shift on, they could still get the benefits of The Shift without the walk problems. So, in theory, a team could simply figure out a way to convince its pitchers to not fall prey to the walk trap and The Shift would once again be their friend.

It's reasonable to think that some teams might be more hip to this idea than others. Maybe some figured it out a year before the others. Maybe they were better at getting the message across to their pitchers. Or, maybe no one has figured it out yet.

Warning! Gory Mathematical Details Ahead!

I used data from 2015-2017, made available through MLB's data portal, Baseball Savant. They are kind enough to note when teams are using an infield shift (three fielders on one side of second base), as opposed to a "strategic shift" (someone's playing a bit out of position, but it's not quite that drastic) or a "standard" alignment.

Since we're doing this by team, I can't just look at raw walk rates, because we know that some teams have good pitchers and others have not-so-good pitchers. Some have a mix of both. I used the log-odds ratio method to take into account a batter's general walking proclivities, and a pitcher's as well, and then shoving them into a binary logistic regression. Then, I asked the computer to generate a specific coefficient for each team's pitchers, for when they went into The Shift and how that affected their walk rate.

Using those coefficients, I was able to project what would happen if a league-average pitcher faced a league-average hitter (which we expect would product a league-average walk rate; from 2015-2017, 7.7 percent of plate appearances ended in a walk) and then just switched his hat. Here's the top five and the bottom five:

Top 5 Teams	Projected Shift Walk Rate	Bottom 5 Teams	Projected Shift Walk Rate
Rockies	6.2%	Rangers	11.2%
Pirates	6.7%	Mets	10.4%
Indians	7.2%	Dodgers	10.2%
Astros	7.3%	Cardinals	9.9%
Braves	7.7%	Tigers	9.7%

There are probably people out there right now trying to figure out what the common thread is among the top and bottom teams. I'm sure, because this is Baseball Prospectus, people are already trying to make the case that sabermetric "early adopters" have some sort of edge here. I think that the more interesting piece is that by the time you get to fifth place in The Shift, we're at league average.

As a sanity check, I examined the issue on a pitch-by-pitch level, looking at how often pitchers threw their pitches in the GameDay strike zone, and again using the same basic methodology and getting team-specific coefficients. The names on the list re-arranged themselves, but the idea was the same, and the two lists correlated with an R of .593.

There's a reason that I don't usually do this type of leaderboard post. I don't really know what the Rockies, Pirates, Indians, Astros, and Braves have in common, or what they have that the bottom five don't. I can put a shrug emoji here and say, "Well, it must be something!" but that seems like a cop-out. Instead, I'd like to present another table and suggest that the table above doesn't even really matter anymore.

Year	League Percent Outside K Zone (Full Shift)	League Percent in K Zone (No Shift)	Difference
2015	54.1%	51.1%	3.0%
2016	53.3%	50.9%	2.4%
2017	52.6%	50.9%	1.7%
2018	52.0%	50.7%	1.3%

The hole in The Shift is fixing itself, and it's coming down really fast league wide. In my earlier work on The Shift, I suggested that until teams stopped having such a huge difference between their out-of-zone rate with and without The Shift on, there would just be too many walks for The Shift to make sense. It seems that all 30 of them have been working toward just that. I once estimated that it takes about 10 years for an idea to filter its way through baseball. At this rate, it looks like teams are going to catch up a lot faster than that. And yeah, they're all saber-smart now.

It's likely that whatever magic it was that the Rockies and Pirates had has made its way to Texas and Queens. Or is at least on its way. And if teams are committing to fixing the walk problem, then it's likely that they will continue shifting and shifting a lot.

And eventually it's going to actually make sense for them to do it.

—Russell Carleton is a former author of Baseball Prospectus and now an analyst for the New York Mets.

The State of the Quality Start

Rob Mains

One of the seven things you (probably) didn't know about the 2018 season is that quality starts—defined as a start lasting six or more innings with three or fewer earned runs allowed—as a percentage of total starts cratered to an all-time low of 41 percent. I want to look a little more deeply into this, since it's been a while (May of 2016, to be exact) since I've examined quality starts.

The term *quality start* is credited to *Philadelphia Inquirer* sportswriter John Lowe. It's been derided ever since he coined it in December of 1985. Three runs in six innings? That's a 4.50 ERA! In what world is that a measure of quality?

Let's start with that criticism. It's true that 3 x 9 / 6 = 4.5. (You came here for this sort of high-level math, right?) But it's also true that type of start, meeting the bare minimum for earning a quality start, is unusual. Here's the proportion of quality starts in which the pitcher lasted exactly six innings and yielded exactly three earned runs. (I'm going to confine this analysis to the 30-team era, 1998-present. Almost all data retrieved in this article is via the Baseball-Reference Play Index.)

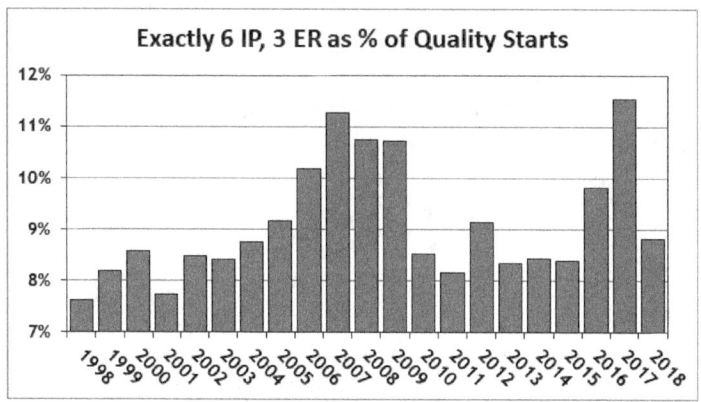

There were 1,997 quality starts in 2018. Only 176, or fewer than one in 11, featured a pitcher going six innings and allowing three earned runs. Put another way, the percentage of quality starts that resulted in a 4.50 ERA (8.8 percent) is less than half the percentage of games in which a batter hit two home runs and his team lost (22.5 percent; 237-69 won-lost). That doesn't impugn hitting two homers.

So if a 4.50 ERA isn't the norm, what is? How good are quality starts? Pretty good, it turns out. First, on a team level:

Teams receiving a quality start from their pitcher won 68.4 percent of their games in 2018, in line with the 30-team era average of 67.9 percent. A team with a .684 winning percentage wins 111 games. Getting a quality start is definitely a good thing. Individual pitchers throwing quality starts have a higher winning percentage because a big slice of team losses is assigned to a reliever.

If teams do well in quality starts, how well do the starting pitchers do? Again, very well.

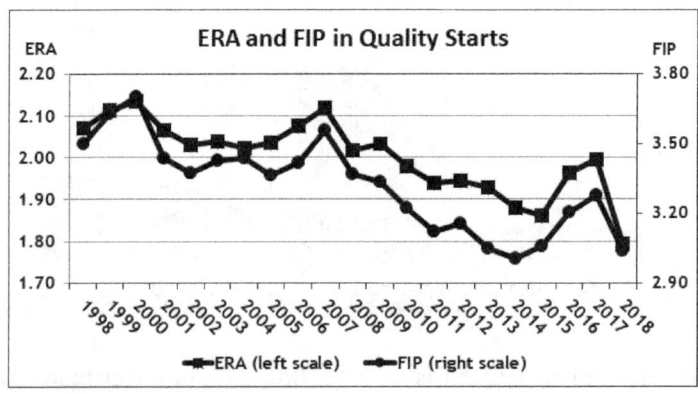

Pitchers in quality starts had a 1.79 ERA (blue line) in 2018, *the lowest in the 30-team era*. Their FIP was higher, 3.04, but still excellent. In the 30-team era, only 2014 had a lower FIP for quality starts, 3.01.

But, of course, the run environment in 2014 was different. Teams in 2014 scored 4.07 runs per game, the fewest in a non-strike year since 1976. They scored 4.45 runs per game in 2018. So surrendering a 3.04 FIP in 2018 is more impressive than 3.01 in 2014. Accordingly, let's look at ERA and FIP in quality starts relative to league averages.

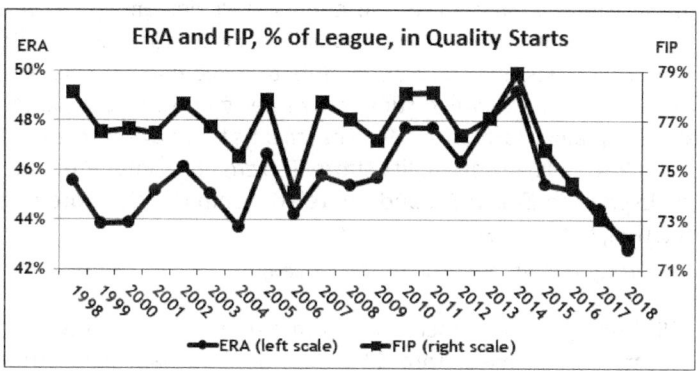

This tells a more dramatic story. Starting pitchers in 2018 gave up a 4.19 ERA and a 4.21 FIP. Starters in quality starts gave up a 1.79 ERA, 43 percent of the league average. Starters in quality starts gave up a 3.04 FIP, 72 percent of the league average. Both of these marks represent lows in the 30-team era.

The takeaway here is this: *Quality starts are better, relative to other starts, than they've ever been over the past 21 years.*

Maybe during the winter I'll look at this over a longer arc of time. For now, though, we can definitively say quality starts are the best they've ever been since the Diamondbacks and Rays joined the majors.

Yet, paradoxically, they're down.

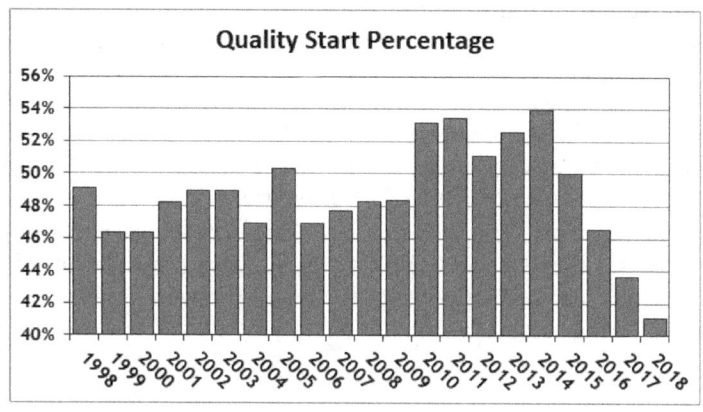

This graph covers only the 30-team era. In my article last week, though, I looked at the years 1908-2018. The result was the same. The 41 percent of starts in 2018 that were quality starts are an all-time low, well below the runners-up: 1930's 43 percent (the year teams scored an all-time record 5.55 runs per game) and last year's 44 percent.

The normal explanation for a dip in quality start percentage is an increase in scoring. When teams score a lot of runs, it's harder for starting pitchers to last six or more innings and limit opponents to three earned runs. From 1998 to 2014, the correlation between runs scored per game and the percentage of starts that were quality starts was -0.94. That means there was an extremely close relationship: More runs, fewer quality starts. Too small a sample? Go back to the start of the Expansion Era, 1961, and the relationship is even more negative, a -0.95 correlation, though 2014.

But that's broken down over the past four years:

- 2015: Runs per game increased from 4.07 to 4.25, quality start percentage decreased from 54.0 to 50.1. Yes, that's a negative relationship, but the regression model would predict a decline of 1.5 percentage points. We got 3.9 instead.
- 2016: Runs per game increased from 4.25 to 4.48, quality start percentage decreased from 50.1 to 46.6. Past experience would suggest a decline of just 1.8 percentage points. We got 3.4.
- 2017: Runs per game increased from 4.48 to 4.65, quality start percentage decreased from 46.6 to 43.6. Again, the direction's right, but the magnitude isn't. Using the relationship from 1998 to 2014, that increase in scoring should've reduced quality starts by 1.3 percentage points, not 2.9.
- 2018: Runs per game declined from 4.65 to 4.45. That should've resulted in the quality start percentage moving in the other direction, rising 1.6 points. It didn't. It fell 2.6 points, as noted, to an all-time low.

Granted, we're talking about just four years here. Maybe they're outliers. But I don't think they are. Quality starts, as noted, are as good or better than ever. But they're rarer than ever as well. And I think I know why.

To get a quality start, you need to allow three or fewer earned and pitch at least six innings. That's 18 outs. Here's a graph showing the number of starting pitchers who limited their opponents to three or fewer earned runs but got pulled after pitching at least five innings but fewer than six:

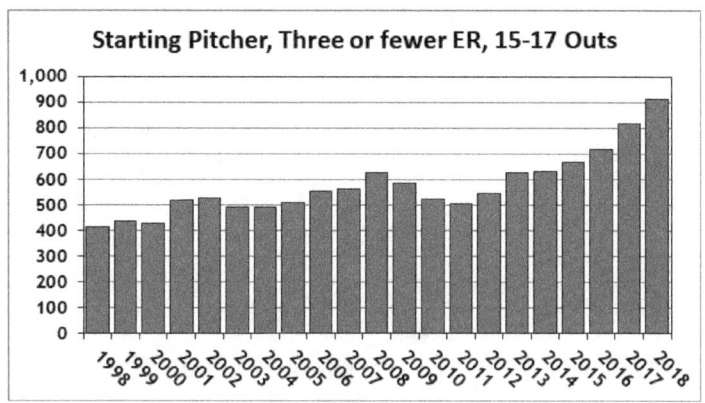

A pitcher getting 15 outs pitched five innings. A pitcher getting 16 outs pitched 5 1/3. A pitcher getting 17 outs pitched 5 2/3. More than ever before, pitchers are being removed from games in which they are within 1-3 outs of a quality start, falling just short of the six-inning finish line. Widespread acknowledgement of the times-through-the-order penalty and a flotilla of available bullpen arms is making the quality start simultaneously both more excellent and more rare.

Which is ironic, given that we saw a new post-war quality start record this season:

Rank	Pitcher	Season	Consecutive QS
1	Jacob deGrom	2018	24
2	Bob Gibson	1968	22
-	Chris Carpenter	2005	22
4	Johan Santana	2004	21
5	Luis Tiant	1968	20
-	Mike Scott	1986	20
-	Jake Arrieta	2015	20
8	Robin Roberts	1952	19
-	Tom Seaver	1973	19
-	Jack Morris	1983	19
-	Greg Maddux	1998	19
-	Josh Johnson	2010	19
-	Jon Lester	2014	19

While there have been longer streaks spread over multiple seasons, no pitcher since World War II threw more consecutive quality starts in one year than Jacob deGrom this year. The fact that he did in a year in which quality starts were the rarest they've ever been adds to the accomplishment.

—*Rob Mains is an author of Baseball Prospectus.*

Heads-Up Hacking—The First Pitch

Matthew Trueblood

Batters fell behind in a higher percentage of all plate appearances in 2018 than in any previous season for which we have pitch-by-pitch data. That kind of granular information goes back only to 1988, but we might safely assume (given all we know about baseball as it had been before that, and as it has been in the years since) that batters have *never* fallen behind at a higher rate than they did last season.

Through the 1990s, the percentage of all plate appearances that began 0-1 hovered in the high 30s and low 40s. In the 2000s, it rose steadily but slowly, through the mid-40s. In 2018, 49.8 percent of all trips to the plate began 0-1. That, as much as anything, captures in microcosm the nature of hitting in MLB today.

A countdown clock toward strike three begins ticking almost the moment a batter takes his place in the box. The league's adjusted OPS+ on the first pitch was higher in 2018 than ever before, and that has been true in most of the last 10 seasons. Batters hit .264/.289/.442 in all plate appearances in which they swung at the first pitch last season, and .241/.330/.395 in all plate appearances in which they took that first offering.

The percentage differences in batting average and isolated power there favor swinging at the first pitch by more than in any season since 1988, while the difference in on-base percentage favors taking by more than ever. If you want to get on base at a decent clip, it's a good idea to be patient, but you run the risk of missing the only chances you'll get to produce power.

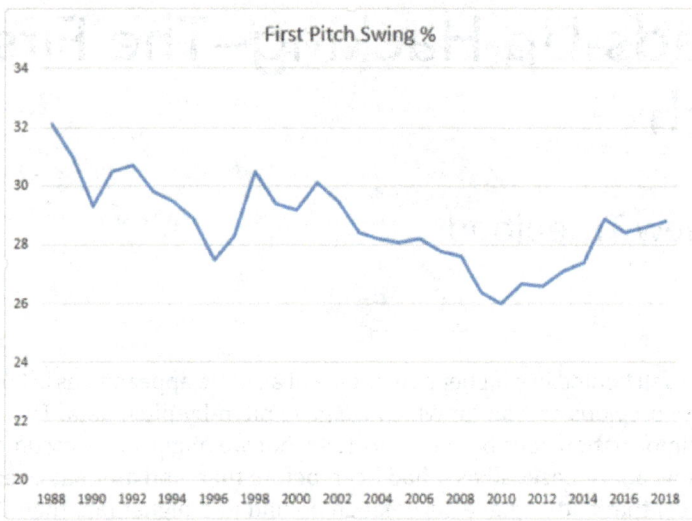

The league swung at the first pitch 28.8 percent of the time in 2018. With the isolated exception of 2015, that's the highest that number has climbed since 2002, but it might not be high enough. With the help of BP research maven Rob McQuown, I looked at the aggregate Called Strike Probability (CSProb) on the first pitch for each season since 2008, when the implementation of PITCHf/x first made measuring that possible. It's risen sharply during that period.

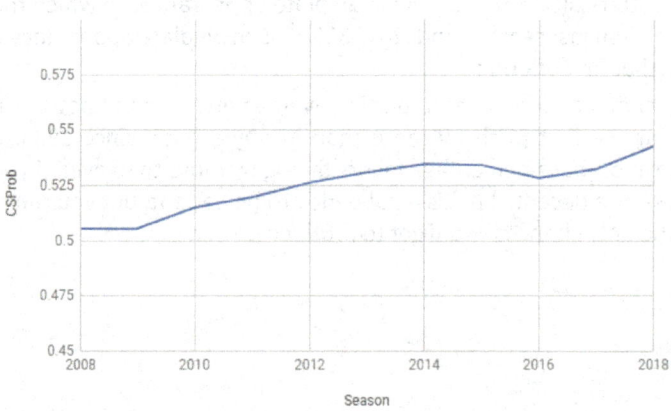

Called Strike Probability, First Pitch of PA (2008-2018)

Called Strike Probability is exactly what it sounds like: a pitch with a given CSProb has roughly that chance of being called a strike, if not swung at. In 2018, a batter who took 100 first pitches from a random sampling of the league's pitchers might expect to fall behind 54 or 55 times—up from 50 or 51 times in 2008. Almost regardless of pitch type (and, notably, especially in the case of fastballs), the first pitch tends to have more of the zone right now than ever before.

Pitchers are better at throwing strikes. They have better stuff, and believe more in their ability to miss bats within the zone. Perhaps most importantly, they know that batters are looking for one thing on the first pitch: a fastball. If they don't get it, they're likely to take the pitch. Check out how the use of sinkers and four-seamers on the first pitch has changed in a decade:

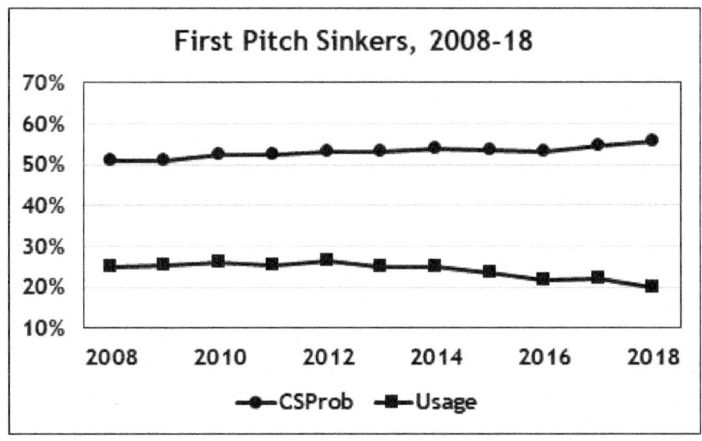

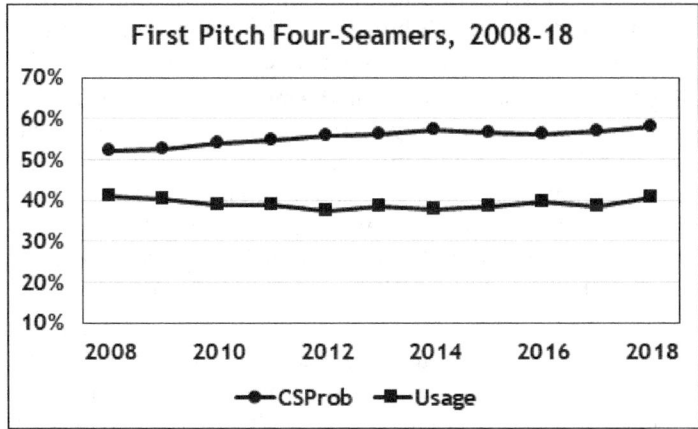

The sinker is losing its place in baseball, but the rate at which pitchers have thrown it on the first pitch hasn't dropped any faster than its usage rate in other counts. Pitchers have actually gone to their four-seamer *more* often to open counts, in the last few years, after a dip in the 2012-2015 period. What's really changed, though, and what shows up in both charts above, is that pitchers are catching more of the zone with first-pitch fastballs than they were a decade ago, or a half-decade ago. They're attacking right away, even with the pitch they know batters are expecting. The message is pretty clear: batters are being too passive.

Sliders, curves, and changeups each have more of the zone when thrown on the first pitch than they did several years ago, too, though the effect is less pronounced. Pitchers have seen the numbers; they know batters are doing better on the first pitch itself. They still feel safe throwing more and better strikes than ever before, figuring they'll come out ahead as long as they keep getting ahead to open each battle.

The Moneyball revolution brought an increased league-wide focus on OBP, which resulted in a de facto mandate to take a more patient tack at the plate. It worked very well for a while, as batters with poor plate discipline were compelled to either adjust or be expelled from the league, and pitchers with poor control were slowly weeded out.

However, concurrent with that revolution, and spurred by it in some ways, was the evolution of the pitching paradigm that now dominates the game. As batters ratcheted up their focus on inflating pitch counts and working walks, pitchers honed theirs on throwing strikes and missing bats. The league's understanding of what makes a good pitcher improved at least as much, from the mid-1990s through the mid-2000s, as its understanding of what makes a good hitter. As amphetamines and other performance-enhancing drugs were phased mostly out of the game, and as PITCHf/x broke onto the scene, individuals and teams learned how to exploit the evolved approaches of even the smartest hitters.

The ability to avoid making outs is still the most valuable one in baseball, but the magnitude of its eclipse of slugging is smaller than ever. To a greater extent than power, on-base skills derive their value from chaining—from the on-base skill levels of the players on either side of a given individual. Eleven years ago, when the housing crisis hit, people learned the hard way that the value of their homes depended a good deal on the values of their neighbors' homes. The same wasn't true, though, of their cars. So it is now, with OBP and SLG.

The global OBP in 2018 was .318. The only seasons since the Dead Ball Era in which the league got on base at a worse clip were 2013-2015, 1988, 1971-1972, and 1963-1968. This is all happening despite the aforementioned evolution of the science of hitting. It's happening despite a shift in approach and focus, one that would steer OBP ever higher, if only it were working.

Instead, it's sitting at a low ebb, and while it does so, even guys who get on base often are a little less helpful than they were 10 years ago—or 20, or 40, or 60, or 70, or 80, or 90. They're less helpful, that is, because unless there happen to be three or four other guys in the lineup who get on just as regularly, their contribution is merely to forestall the inevitable. Runs happen, increasingly, when a sudden bang happens, and that means attacking early in the count—because pitchers are sure as hell doing that.

In a league making contact on barely 75 percent of its swings, and a league in which an increasing number of pitchers can throw multiple off-speed pitches for strikes in any count, the only way to consistently generate offense is going to be aggressive. This isn't necessarily true for individuals, like Mookie Betts and Jose Ramirez, who make a lot of contact and have excellent plate discipline, and whose power comes from such natural quickness in a short stroke. Most players have to make tradeoffs, though, whether it be lowering their contact rate or raising their chase rate, in order to consistently make the quality of contact necessary to survive in today's game.

Highest %	Lowest %
Javier Baez – 48.3	Joe Mauer – 4.6
Freddie Freeman – 47.1	Mookie Betts – 9.7
Ozzie Albies – 46.3	Brett Gardner – 10.7
Jose Altuve – 44.2	Jose Ramirez – 12.0
Nick Castellanos – 44.1	Jason Kipnis – 13.8
Joey Gallo – 42.3	Jesus Aguilar – 14.5
Corey Dickerson – 40.9	Xander Bogaerts – 15.8
Salvador Perez – 40.8	Brian Dozier – 16.3
Eddie Rosario – 40.7	Mike Trout – 17.6
Nick Ahmed – 40.4	Yasmani Grandal – 17.6

Top 10 and Bottom 10 Hitters, First-Pitch Swing Rate (2018)

The question isn't which of these lists one prefers, but what they each convey, qualitatively, about the cat-and-mouse game of early-count hitting. Those top five on the left, especially, drive home the fact that for most players, getting aggressive early in the count is now key to keeping strikeout rate down and hitting for power.

For now, the message is: pitchers are coming right after batters with the nastiest stuff they've ever had. Batters had better stop giving away strike one and force hurlers to adjust, or the global OBP crisis is only going to get worse.

—*Matthew Trueblood is an author of Baseball Prospectus.*

A Hymn for the Index Stat

Patrick Dubuque

We survived without computers. I know this, because I remember the day when my dad hooked up his brand-new Atari 400 computer to the back of our 12-inch Magnavox television, and the perfect blue of the memo pad lit up for the first time. I was born just on the edge of that transitional generation, of learning cursive and balancing checkbooks and just doing math all the time, constant manual arithmetic.

It still amazes me. We learned how to sail ships without computers. We learned how to do calculus. We built towers that didn't fall down, most of the time. We engineered catapults to knock them down anyway. We built a robust system of philosophy called "utilitarianism," founded on the principle that the good of an action is evaluated by summing the effects of that action, which is the kind of formula that would make the world's mainframes crash. The whole foundation of statistics as a field is "here's math you could easily do but would die of old age first."

The fact of the matter is that there is too much math in the world to do. There are too many things changing, and too many things too small to notice, for us to handle. At some point, they become too much for the computers to handle as well, which is why we have chaos theory and undetectable earthquakes, but it's not an even fight. At some point, we fall back on intuition, and given how under-equipped we are, we're forced to bestow that intuition with some sort of supernatural superiority, the "gut feeling," that we can't prove because we can only intuit that our intuition is better.

We're all lousy at intuition, and wonderful at lying to ourselves about it. The honest truth is that computers are far better at intuition than we are, because in order to know what feels "off" you have to know what's "on." In order to do that you have to constantly reassess the average of everything, then re-rank your own experience against it.

Test your own, by comparing these three anonymous lines:

Player	G	HR	AVG	OBP	SLG
Player A	156	38	.259	.342	.535
Player B	154	38	.280	.348	.527
Player C	158	38	.266	.343	.509

These all seem like pretty similar players, right? The second one a touch more batted-ball dependent, the third a little less strong, but all pretty good hitters. And you'd be right, about the latter. Not the former.

Here's the breakdown:

- Player A: 1991 Howard Johnson, 141 DRC+
- Player B: 1996 Dean Palmer, 121 DRC+
- Player C: 2018 Giancarlo Stanton, 114 DRC+

Baseball is fortunate to have escaped the seismic shifts of so many other sports, where the talents and performances of other eras are nearly unrecognizable. (And not just other sports: try to explain the greatness of the movie Duck Soup without adjusting for era.) But they're still there, and they're nearly impossible to account for manually, without having to resort to sweeping generalizations like "steroid era" or juiced-ball era" to throw out entire swathes of production.

This is all to say that we should celebrate the index stat, that simple 100-based scale with such a humble aim: just to give context. It's hard to imagine how we lived without them for so long. Sabermetricians have always tried to make their stats look like other stats: True Average mapped to batting average, FIP molded to look like and compare to ERA. It's easy to understand the motivation—these statistics carry an emotional value in them that is hard to resist, as with the .300 hitter and the 2.00 ERA—but even they fall prey to the same loss of scale as their unadjusted counterparts. If a .300 average means different things in different years, does that hold true for a .300 True Average?

Instead, 100 doesn't say anything, except above average or below. And it does it instantly, for every season in every run environment for any statistic we want it to. We should have more index stats: K%+, so we can stop comparing Mike Clevinger's career 9.46 K/9 to Nolan Ryan's 9.55. HBP%+, so we can note that Ron Hunt was getting plunked when nobody else was getting plunked, as opposed to that imitator Brandon Guyer. Some might note how stale these references are and accuse league-adjustment as a backward-looking drive, and this is true. But we're always looking backward, always comparing the new with the expectations already set. The index stat just forces us to be honest.

There's always resistance to a new statistic, especially one so outwardly simple and so internally complex. We tend to stick with what we know, even in the case of formulas that are supposed to tell us what we know. But if your resistance is that it seems too complicated, too counterintuitive, too "black boxy," I encourage you to consider why you feel that way. Because the real world is infinitely more complicated than baseball, where all the pitches go in one basic direction and the baserunners are only allowed to travel in four directions. Baseball statistics based on mixed methodology are almost impossibly intricate. So are skyscrapers and automobiles. That's why we have computers—to take the guesswork out of them.

—*Patrick Dubuque is an author of Baseball Prospectus.*

Index of Names

Adcock, Brett 90
Adolph, Ross 89, 101
Altuve, Jose 18
Alvarez, Jose 89
Alvarez, Yordan 78, 95
Arauz, Jonathan 89, 101
Armenteros, Rogelio 83, 100
Beer, Seth 79, 98
Bielak, Brandon 90
Brantley, Michael 20
Bregman, Alex 22
Bukauskas, J.B. 84, 96
Chirinos, Robinson 24
Cole, Gerrit 48
Correa, Carlos 26
Deetz, Dean 90
Devenski, Chris 50
Diaz, Aledmys 28
Fisher, Derek 30
Guduan, Reymin 90
Gurriel, Yulieski 32
Harris, Will 52
Hartman, Ryan 90
Ivey, Tyler 90
James, Josh 54, 95
Jaquez, Ernesto 90
Javier, Cristian 90
Kemp, Tony 34
Marisnick, Jake 36
Martes, Francis 85
Martin, Corbin 86, 97
Matijevic, J.J. 89
McCullers, Lance 56
McHugh, Collin 58
McKenna, Alex 89, 102
Miley, Wade 60
Nova, Freudis 80, 97
Osuna, Roberto 62
Peacock, Brad 64
Perez, Cionel 66, 99
Pineda, Andy 89
Pressly, Ryan 68
Reddick, Josh 38
Reed, A.J. 81
Rodgers, Brady 90
Rondon, Hector 70
Santana, Luis 89, 100
Schroeder, Jayson 90
Smith, Joe 72
Solis, Jairo 87, 102
Springer, George 40
Stassi, Max 42
Straw, Myles 82
Stubbs, Garrett 89
Toro, Abraham 89, 102
Tucker, Kyle 44, 94
Valdez, Framber 74, 99
Verlander, Justin 76
White, Tyler 46
Whitley, Forrest 88, 93

Ballpark diagrams for Baseball Prospectus are created by THIRTY81Project, a design concept offering original ballpark artwork, including the new 'Ballparks of 2019' 11 x 17 color print.

Visit **www.thirty81project.com** for full details.

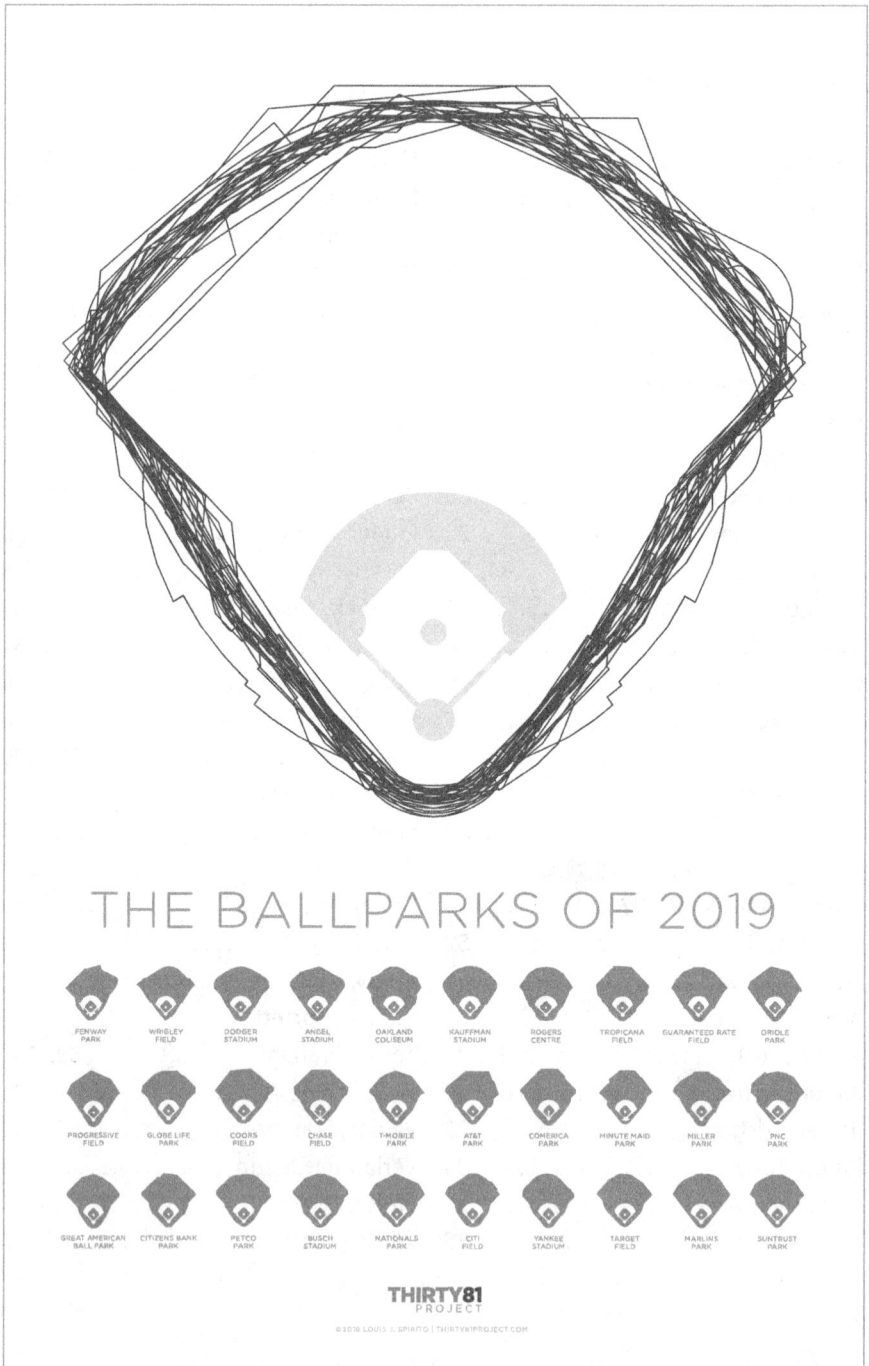